Tarot – The Life Code

By Janis King

What People Are Saying About

Tarot – The Life Code

It is always exciting to see traditional practices evolve, and *Tarot – The Life Code* seems to be doing just that by offering a fresh perspective on reading Tarot and understanding the cards. The idea of linking the majors to specific suits is intriguing. Its encouraging to encounter innovative approaches like this that can help an enthusiast grow their Tarot skills and expand interpretations.

Kim Arnold, UK Tarot Conference and author

Looking for a new way to use the Tarot cards that features fortune-creating instead of fortune-telling? This book might be for you. It presents a new matrix system for manifesting what you desire by using the four suits of the Minor Arcana to map your progress and the Major Arcana to give you guidance along the way.

Mary K. Greer, author and Tarot academic

Tarot – The Life Code

A Fool, a Magician, and the Secret of Life

by Janis King

BOOKS

London, UK

Washington, DC, USA

First published by O-Books, 2025
O-Books is an imprint of Collective Ink Ltd.,
Unit 11, Shepperton House, 89 Shepperton Road, London, N1 3DF
office@collectiveinkbooks.com
www.collectiveinkbooks.com
www.o-books.com

For distributor details and how to order, please visit the 'Ordering' section on our website.

ISBN: 978 1 80341 780 6
978 1 80341 981 7 (ebook)
Library of Congress Control Number: 2024948009

A CIP catalogue record for this book is available from the British Library.

Design: Lapiz Digital Services

UK: Printed and bound by CPI Group (UK) Ltd, Croydon, CR0 4YY
Printed in North America by CPI GPS partners

With fond memories of Ray and Anna and our Tarot 'come dine with me' journey.

Contents

Preface

This is not a 'learn to read Tarot' book. This is a book to help you experience Tarot differently, in a way that will eventually make perfect sense and deepen the quality of your readings. I will show you why you should put aside just learning individual card meanings and see Tarot for what it really is – an overall explanation of how life works, and that every single human experience is held within it. Delving into it is to be constantly amazed; there is always more to discover and explore. There are stories that run like a river through every part of the Tarot and this is my focus when I teach or give talks about Tarot.

The Life Code will contribute to the process of us seeing and experiencing Tarot as an important component in our desire to raise our consciousness, and I hope this book will help your awareness of the potential of Tarot beyond its role as an oracle. Instead, I see it as an instruction manual for a system that can help you become creative with your life energy.

Over the last decade Tarot has grown enormously in popularity, as a source of wisdom available to anyone looking for help, clarity or guidance. It has an uncanny ability to get to the heart of any issue, offering tremendous insight with no agenda and no direct affiliation with any other area of spiritual work. In the right hands, the insights and guidance it provides have benefited thousands of people, many who would never consider themselves alternative or 'woo woo' in the least. Its use has become less stigmatised and it is now being recognised for its effectiveness in counselling and as a therapeutic tool. Its profile has been slowly but steadily climbing, elevated beyond its historically notorious reputation as a risky purveyor of potentially unwelcome news. The dark, apparently scary 'movie star' archetypes of Tarot – Death, the Lovers, the Tower and the Hanged Man – whose reputations have fed into the rhetoric around Tarot as a slightly dangerous dance with the dark side, are now more widely understood and viewed with much less trepidation. This has allowed the use of Tarot to become normalised to the point where it is potentially ready to step forward as a spiritual path in its own right.

The idea of a spiritual path being non-religious is being embraced and championed by a new wave of those who are open-minded, curious and interested in change. They are collectively redefining our understanding of relationships, both to each other and to ourselves. It gives us a link between the psychology of our emotions and our spiritual energy. Non-judgemental, non-discriminatory and not planted in any one culture, it connects and elevates humanity through a common language that understand communal suffering.

We all suffer heartache, we all have ambitions, we all struggle with overthinking and a fear of being judged. We all worry about the future while struggling to let go of the past. We are all connected emotionally and energetically, and Tarot speaks to that shared experience. It gives us a way to elevate the experience while still allowing us to be what we are at our core — human. Little by little, Tarot can help make our lives lighter, more elevated and more enriched, not by removing ourselves from the temptations of life, but by living it to the full, with all it has to offer, from the deepest depths of our worst misery to the pinnacles of elation.

All experiences are valuable with the caveat that we are not here to suffer. If you are suffering, then adjustments need to be made. The mix is wrong, that is all. The wonderful part is, that when one person makes those changes, we all benefit. Our outlook, our attitude, the way we acknowledge each other changes things for everyone as we become more spiritualised by default, living increasingly from a position of love and understanding.

Chapter 1

White Dove

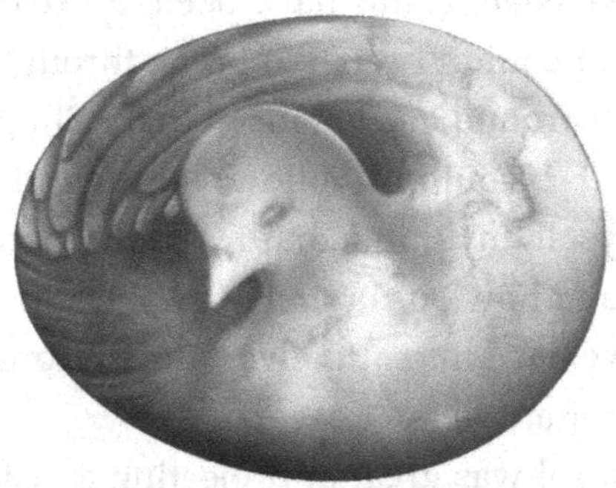

My beginnings with Tarot, and what ultimately inspired me to write this book (and create The Life Code deck), came about in answer to a very specific request, and was the beginning of a long process of discovery. Looking back it all makes perfect sense, but at the time it was hugely challenging.

Many years before I began my relationship with Tarot I grew more and more interested in the idea of being able to 'call' things. This was back in the early 1990s, long before the term 'manifestation' was popularised. It wasn't related to any specific philosophy; in fact, I really did not have any. I had been given a cassette tape (yes, I am that old) by a friend with a simple visualisation technique on it called 'the Pink Bubble'. I fell in love with it and got into testing it. I found I was naturally really good at going into trance (something my teachers at school would agree with). I had some specific successes, however nothing seemed to stick or gain any real momentum. Even so, I remained interested in the process, how it worked and why my results were so patchy and what was going wrong. I figured out that the problem must be me.

On reflection, I realised that I had constantly self-sabotaged; I actually had some incredible opportunities come my way, but something had always prevented me from taking them up. I could see my part though, and how, in retrospect, I had basically backed away every time I was put in front of an opportunity that would have been, could have been, a dream come true. I was in the way. I couldn't seem to break through what felt like an invisible wall around me. I realised that calling opportunities was pointless if I couldn't follow through. I wanted more control over myself, my mind, and my fear. I became interested in psychology and how our brains work. I wanted to know how much control we have in reality over our subconscious minds. I was searching for answers.

The truth was, I was great at projecting a vision of a person full of optimism and confidence, yet underneath I had nothing to stand on. All that surface bravado and determination would sneak away and fail me when I needed real confidence. I would find a reason to back away, convinced that others would see the 'real' me, and realise they had made a terrible mistake. Underneath, I didn't feel like the person they thought I was. I also consistently attracted people into my life who bullied, criticised, and dominated me. I responded by telling myself I just needed to get stronger, tough it out and try to love them more so they would eventually have to love me back. But guess what? None of it worked!

I am telling you this because I want you to know what gave me my own solid foundation, on which everything else was built. I see this story replayed again and again in my work with clients now.

I decided on an experiment. I would put all my 'calling' powers to the test, thinking that the problem with my 'calling' was that I was asking for the wrong things. I decided that I obviously did not know what the right things were, so I decided to try and change things (which also included improving/

saving my marriage) by relinquishing control and asking for something completely different.

'Give me what I need to make everything alright.'

My energy reset would be to serve in some way, and at the back of my mind I had the idea of starting an independent grassroots record company that would promote female artists.

I showed up with this each and every day before I started work. Over the next year, I meditated and made my request — every day.

'Give me what I need to make everything alright.'

Over time I shortened that to 'give me what I need'. I then said thank you, and got on with the day.

And it worked, with amazing results!

The energy was supercharged. People and situations moved into place, as if magically orchestrated. Things began working in a way they never had. I signed a high-profile client, and everything went smoothly for about 18 months.

Then, just like that, within a 48-hour period, everything hit the deck.

My client became increasingly erratic, other contracts weren't honoured, lawsuits were threatened, and everything that had seemed so perfect was shattered. Our finances were in tatters, my marriage was breaking, I was in shock. My husband and I lost our house and, ultimately, we split up. I was broken, hit the floor and couldn't get back up. I went into a major depression and had what was in effect a breakdown.

I was sitting in my car one day, when the reality of it first hit me, hard. I started to cry almost convulsively — worse than I had ever cried before (and believe me I've shed my share of tears). As I cried, things started spiralling and spinning, and I felt as if I was falling into a deep, bottomless black hole. I did then what many people do when they hit ground zero, I started ranting at God. Yet, even though my interest in energy and the energetic world was long-standing, it was never religious. That day though, with nowhere to go, broke, no career, heartbroken and lost, I went straight to the head guy.

I know, 'head guy', don't shoot me, eh?

It's not because I think God is actually a guy, just that it was the pronoun that felt immediately familiar and carried the most authority. I had never much been into the idea of God but, yes, that day, like we do, I took it all out on 'him'. I could no longer see a future. I had run out of everything. I just could not believe it, my faith in everything I had believed in had failed, my experiment had proved to be complete fantasy – I had no power, it had all been an illusion.

I poured it all out, all my pain, right there in the car. That it felt so unfair, that I'd tried so hard, done my best – that we all do our absolute best down here, working so hard but still we screw up or it goes wrong, and we get so much pain and suffering, and we've no idea what to do; we get no real help at all.

I said, 'how are we supposed to know what to do? There's no instruction manual. Why can't we have a map of some kind? Something to help us know how to do life!'

I felt completely alone and adrift. I didn't know how to move forward, where to go. I vented everything until I ran out of steam.

Then, out loud, I asked the question, 'should I give up, or should I just have faith that there's a way forward?'

As I said the words 'have faith', I heard another voice say it with me. It overlaid my own. I heard it so clearly it actually made me jump. I was so stunned, that my tears stopped mid flow and everything went very quiet.

After a few seconds, I actually replied, rather suspiciously, saying, 'okay, voice, whoever you are, I heard that, but I need a bit more than that, thank you very much. What should I have faith in?'

No answer came, just silence. But the emotional storm had passed and I did feel calmer. I carried on meditating, fruitlessly it seemed, trying to get in contact with my guides. God had always felt to me as if 'he' was behind the emergency glass, not to be bothered except when there was a fire of some kind. I knew I should have guides – other people talked about theirs, but mine seemed nowhere to be found. Guides seemed a bit like celestial line managers, the help line that should be available for problem solving. The CEO (God) was probably upstairs doing the important stuff in an important office dealing with important problems, not to be bothered unless really, really necessary. But it seemed to me at that time that customer service needed a serious rethink.

Maybe, I thought, I was in a kind of energetic call-waiting line: 'thank you for calling, we know you are waiting. We're experiencing a high volume of calls right now and all of the guides are busy. Please continue to hold?'

A month or so later, on one of my daily meditations, I asked again to meet with a guide to show me the way forward, I'd been doing this for a while but that day something different happened. As I sat in the meditation, I found myself sitting on a bench with flat fields either side and a wood in the distance. A small boy ran out of the wood and sat next to me. He was about 8 years old, dressed in shorts and a blue and white stripy T-shirt. His feet were bare. He had golden skin and sandy-coloured hair, and he kicked his legs and fidgeted. He was also blind; his eyes sealed shut, although he didn't seem to mind. I asked him if he was a guide, but he shook his head and handed to me what looked like a white stone egg. Carved into it was a curled-up sleeping bird and I said, *oh, it's a white dove*. The boy nodded and ran off, leaving me mystified. Again, no clear answers, and more silence.

A couple of weeks later, just before Christmas, I was wandering around Camden Market and spotted a kind of hippy shop called Rainbow Visions. It advertised 'Tarot Readings' in the window and it looked interesting so I decided to check it out. Inside, a guy with long white hair, dressed in white robes, sat in a small office at the back reading for someone, and I asked the man at the counter about a reading.

He said, 'you need to speak to White Dove, but he's reading for someone at the moment.'

White Dove — I thought, *seriously*?

So I knew I needed to book a reading, and the reading I had with White Dove, whom I still know, changed my life.

He told me I was in the middle of a karmic storm, and that my life was being fundamentally taken apart and put back together. It would be a challenging journey, but I would be supported by 'angels' along the path when I needed it. It seemed that my call to 'give me what I need' had been heard and was being implemented. He also told me I was being moved to a different path. I told him no way and, if so, I'd changed my mind. I took it all back and didn't want any of this. I didn't want a different path, I was a musician and that's what I wanted. It was part of my 'make it alright' picture; I had pretty much lost everything else, I couldn't lose that as well.

He told me it made no difference, it was happening anyway and I should allow it to take its course. He didn't say what that new path was, only that I would find out, when the time was right. He also told me that my (ex) husband had unconditional love for me, that it didn't matter now but I should remember it later. It felt like another blow in this very unfunny celestial joke. What exactly, in this picture, should I have faith in?

I left with a set of instructions about how to deal with the next three years, which he again warned me were going to be hard. He was right, but there were angels as he promised, although of a very human kind.

That was many years ago. The journey from that reading was full of adventure, heartbreak and some incredible miracles – another story for another time, perhaps?

The important thing for this book is that my journey with Tarot began that day. I started my relationship with this mysterious source of information because of my reading with White Dove and started to find my way to the path I had been guided to.

From the beginning of my Tarot journey, I loved the way the cards worked as a pictorial language that enabled me to have a conversation. I spoke to the cards and they spoke back. They had a very specific voice: calm, down to earth and matter of fact. I had no idea whom I was talking to, but there seemed very clearly to be an intelligence on the other end, one that definitely had a mind of its own and even on occasion a wry sense of humour, putting me in my place when the need arose.

I spent the first five years of our 'relationship' slightly freaked out by this voice that replied in pictorial form through the cards. But as my knowledge of the language improved, so did my trust in my disembodied friend. Whomever was on the end of the line, I found that I liked them, and we grew to understand each other better as our communication improved.

We are physical, they are not, but they want to help as best they can because it's not easy here in the physical world. Their advice always allows for our free will. This life is our gift, it is ours to do with as we wish, any way we choose. We can draw on their advice, always available, but we can also make our own choices. In fact, though, I have felt as if *The Life Code* is actually a message directly from them. It has felt as if they were using this book to communicate, as they use Tarot when we speak during my readings for clients. This book is them saying what they want to say, about life and how we can best go about it.

But this book is not about them, it is about us and our individual journeys. It starts with us in the Tarot deck as well, because that's what I believe the Fool and the Magician represent: us, in energetic and physical forms.

Chapter 2

The Language of Tarot

In my early days experimenting with energy and meditation, I was often frustrated when trying to reach and communicate with my spirit guides, as my clients are often frustrated when they try to reach theirs.

It appears to me from my readings now, that there is also some frustration in the energetic world as it tries to convey information to us through the static of our mental and emotional noise. To bypass this, the energetic world needs a simple communication system, a shared language. Ideally, something that can talk to us through our intuition but which we can understand subconsciously. Using this mechanism, they would be able to communicate through a network of 'open' individuals who deliver messages and who could teach others, making communication between physical and spiritual more common and the information and lessons offered more widely accepted. They (the spiritual) could help more people using spiritual teachings from across the globe, adaptable to any appropriate language. It should not be owned or controlled by anyone, no one source should be able to claim it, and it should not be something that would fall within the doctrine of a specific religion that would want to control access to it. It should be completely of the people. I believe Tarot is that language.

Using playing cards as the foundation for the universal language meant that a specific pictorial code could be developed, one that could be learned. It is a more grounded, more accessible means of communication than other forms of energetic communication. As it has developed it has become more finely tuned to us spiritually and physically, making communication completely possible for anyone who chooses to learn the language.

Tarot became the answer through its energetic evolution, although the exact history and folklore around its origin is rather shrouded in mystery. We know that Tarot appeared in the western world in the fourteenth century – where it came from before that we can only speculate.

Some believe Tarot comes from ancient Egypt, others believe it originates in tenth-century China; some believe it is of Islamic origin, others see roots in Indian culture or to the mystic system of the Kabbalah.

Even the name Tarot itself adds to the confusion. The name may originate from the ancient Egyptian words *tar ro* meaning 'the royal road'. But we also have *taru,* Hindu for 'sacred tree', and *tara* the mother goddess from both Hinduism and Buddhism. In Hinduism, tara is a form of the female primordial energy known as *shakti*. In Buddhism, she is female. Or perhaps its name is of Hebrew origin as the holy book the *Torah,* the first five books of the Old Testament. Perhaps it's perfectly apt that we can't pin it down. The name Tarot is all of the above, encapsulating our varying descriptions of a higher path, of higher knowledge and of a universal source of energy that we have been trying to connect with for all time.

As described, the symbolism in the cards doesn't bow to any one source or culture but draws its wisdom from spiritual practices across the globe and across human space and time; this is part of its legacy and its power. It is continually evolving and responding, refining both its message and its method of communication.

The cards themselves seem to have their roots in the more human, down to earth pursuit of gambling and card games. They are essentially, at their core, of the people, passed from culture to culture. The Roma people who were most instrumental in this were those known (because they were originally believed to be from Egypt) as Gypsies. They travelled with a specific card game used primarily for gambling known as *Faro*. These cards had painted kings as part of their design and the name is probably a reduction of the word pharaoh or king. The Roma people were not originally from Egypt at all though, they had migrated from the Punjab and Rajasthan regions of India where cards depicting the Hindu god Vishnu and his ten avatars embodying certain soul qualities are still evident today in Tarot's Major Arcana figures and likely inspired them.

It also was the Roma who brought the cards into esoteric use with the practice of fortune telling, called cartomancy. They carried with them the culturally core belief, still inherent at the heart of modern Tarot, that each person is intrinsically divine, that the purpose of life is to seek and realise the divinity within all of us and that God and knowledge is within the self. It may have been this belief, with its roots in Hindu/Eastern philosophy that caused the Church to immediately denounce the cards, perhaps because this message challenged the authority of the Church itself. In reality, whether this was because of links with divination or (more probably) because cards were associated with gambling is not clear, but it has ensured that Tarot has always existed outside the gates of mainstream spirituality or formalised religion — exactly as required.

When the Gypsies arrived in Europe, probably through Italy in the fourteenth century, four suit playing cards were already in existence. One early pattern still used today was the suits of Batons, Coins, Cups and Swords, (Clubs, Diamonds, Hearts and Spades) and it is likely the 'trumps' were added from a separate system, ultimately becoming the deck that was used to play the game *Tarocchi*.

The Tarot of Marseilles is acknowledged as the first 'official' deck of esoteric Tarot, with a movement that started in France with Antoine Court and Jean-Baptiste Alliette (Etteilla as he was known) in Paris during the 1780s. Its underground popularity started to grow as not just a 'Gypsy' fortune-telling myth but also as a genuine mystery of interest to be studied and developed. The

Tarot of Marseilles deck more comfortably reflects the cultural spiritual/religious understanding of the period, creating a more Christian interpretation of the original Eastern images.

Tarot found its next stage of evolution in Great Britain in 1909 with the members of The Hermetic Order of the Golden Dawn and their study of divine magick and spiritual development. The Golden Dawn became one of the largest single influences on twentieth-century western occultism. Our understanding of Tarot today is built primarily from that reworking of the deck by two influential Golden Dawn members, British poet and scholarly mystic, Arthur Edward Waite, and artist, Pamela Colman-Smith. Their reshaping of the Tarot deck softened the more overtly Christian images into the version we are now familiar with and has defined modern Tarot with its rich symbolism and clear structure.

Waite and Colman-Smith saw the study of magick not as a means to power or divination but as a path towards a higher consciousness. Their interpretation of the Tarot system had its emphasis on symbolism and its connection to intuition, personal power and self-actualisation. Pamela Colman-Smith, who was introduced to the Golden Dawn by the poet Yeats, worked with Waite to refine a set of images for this new version of the Tarot. They also created specific images for each of the 'pip' cards (this term refers to a card with a number and suit icons only) as we see on traditional playing cards. The images Colman-Smith created represented the meaning of each card as described by the numerical and energetic (suits) value. The images contained scenes of people experiencing different aspects of life; images that were infused with symbolic clues guiding the reader towards the information symbolised by each card.

Together they distilled the Tarot into a usable, understandable, more logical system, bringing the history and folklore at the root of Tarot into line with the teachings of the Golden Dawn and its philosophy.

Most decks today are created around three versions: the original Tarot of Marseilles; the Rider Waite Smith Deck; and Thoth, a reworking of the RWS deck by Aleister Crowley with illustrations by Lady Frieda Harris.

Thoth drew heavily on the Egyptian symbolism associated with early Tarot and has a slightly different structure to what has become accepted as the standard RWS deck, with renamed Major Arcana cards, traditional 'pip' cards, and with numbers and suits rather than imagery throughout the Minor Arcana and a differing system of Royal dignitaries. Crowley also felt that Waite and Colman-Smith had not gone far enough in de-Christianising the deck, which he felt should fall outside the direct influence of any one religious influence.

So, Tarot has evolved alongside us, transcending geographical, philosophical and spiritual borders. With wisdom and symbolism from all of our greatest spiritual practices grafted onto what was originally common playing cards, Tarot has become a metaphor of human life. It is a conversation from spirit to mankind and back again. It is owned by no one, it has no leaders or prophets, it demands neither allegiance nor obedience. It grows and develops with us through the centuries, into an ever more refined and interactive conversation about our everyday lives with the energetic world.

Discovering the Life Code Deck

I started my relationship with Tarot, as many of us do, with a deck of the Rider Waite Smith cards which are, for many of us, the industry standard around which most modern decks are constructed.

Fast forward a decade later, when I had been working as a Tarot professional for more than a decade, but I could not shake an odd feeling that I was missing something.

My very dear friend, Gayle Joubert, also an energy worker and healer, had just returned from a trip to Bali, where she had been introduced to a spiritual teacher called Per. He had mentioned The Arthur Findlay College in Stansted and she suggested we both go on the first course that had availability. That turned out to be a five-day residential trance mediumship course.

The experience changed everything I thought I knew about working with spirit and the non-physical Realm. I came back supercharged with what felt like electrical energy.

Lying in the bath one day, I suddenly heard a loud voice saying: 'Write the book'. I had been toying with the idea (of a book about Tarot) but was not clear on what I would say. I didn't want to repeat what had already been written, but as the instruction to 'write the book' was delivered, an initial chapter just downloaded into my head.

Really? Right now?

I jumped out of the bath and, barely dry, opened my laptop and started manically typing. I typed what was (broadly speaking) the story you have just read, about how my journey with Tarot began. Then as quickly as it came, it went. I had nothing else to say. Silence followed. Grr, it's so annoying when they do this! I had no idea what on earth I should do next. I felt really frustrated and a bit irritated. I was all fired up with nowhere to go. I've always found the silence between cryptic messages difficult to deal with.

I parked the book and time passed until a few weeks later I paid a visit to my son, Laurie, and his partner, Rhi. Laurie is a writer and board-game designer. Because of who his mama is, almost by default, he also has a working knowledge of Tarot and we were talking about how he visualises game layouts. We started playing with a deck, laying the cards on the floor to create different designs.

We were having fun and got quite into one idea, deciding to make a star. We put the Major Arcana around in a circle (because it is, in essence, a continuing process). He then said that the Minor Arcana should make the points of the star.

'What goes first?' he asked.

'Cups', I said. 'That definitely goes first.'

What's the opposite of Cups? Obviously, Swords, so we put that point opposite the Cups point. What goes between them? It has to be Wands! The suit of Pentacles was then in the final position just by default.

It felt quite arbitrary but as we jiggled the points over the Major Arcana circle, we realised if we took out the Fool and the Magician, the four points sat nice and neatly over the remaining twenty Major Arcana cards. Five cards each in four different sections and, with that, a clear, unexpected picture emerged. The four elements in order, each one building on the next and working in a way I had never seen. The Major Arcana now appeared to work as four distinct areas that fitted nicely with the Minor suits: Emotional/Water (Cups), Energy/Fire (Wands), Mind/Air (Swords) and Experience/Earth (Pentacles).

I felt strangely excited about the whole thing, yet while the layout definitely worked, we couldn't see the connection quickly enough. I really wanted to see those different areas linked visually in some way to make them connect properly.

That was the day The Life Code deck was born. Together with my good friend, fellow Tarot reader and academic, Ray Mallaney, the next few months were spent brainstorming ideas. While we built the deck on the structure laid out by the Rider Waite Smith system, I wanted to convey more literal pictorial representations of how the cards showed up for me in readings with real people; to take the picture-book idea to a new level. So we worked together, re-conceptualising the symbolism we knew and loved into literal, real-life interpretations for each card.

That all worked beautifully and rather magically with the fact my friend Gayle (the 'energetic postman', as I now see her) then asked me to write an advanced level Tarot/self-development course for a specific client of hers who was looking for a teacher. I was resistant to the idea, and felt I had enough on my plate already, but she was insistent that I should do it right away and, because Gayle is my friend, I agreed.

The Life Code system that I had just worked out became the basis for the course, and the course formed the foundation for this book. As I wrote the course, more and more connections started to appear within the system.

After the initial instruction to write a book, the process of writing the course meant that I had to delve more deeply into the idea of the Realms. This began a process of discovery that gained a life of its own. I was being given mechanisms to uncover the actual content one piece at a time as I needed it.

It was created energetically, and that is at the heart of everything. The whole system is built around the premise that we are the Magicians in our own lives and by learning to work together with the universal energies at our disposal we can master ourselves and our lives, creating positive and exciting adventures that make our journeys more awesome.

Here is The Life Code guiding star exactly as it was out on the floor that day:

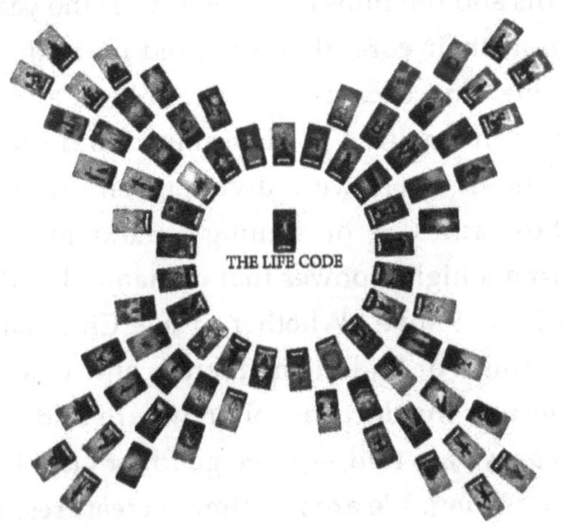

And it turns out, this is the book I was asked to write in the bath, at the beginning of the entire process. Hope you enjoy it!

Chapter 3

The Tarot as a Bible

There is an indefinable mysterious power that pervades everything, I feel it though I do not see it. It is this unseen power which makes itself felt and yet defies all proof, because it is so unlike all that I perceive through my senses. It transcends the senses. Mahatma Ghandi

As I previously mentioned, I look at the Tarot as a kind of holy book – a bible in a way, but a different kind. The word bible comes from the ancient Greek for 'book, paper or scroll on which are written sacred religious scriptures or authority on a specific subject'. I see Tarot as the bible of 'how to do life'; a blueprint or a methodology for creating a life experience of our choosing.

When going through my own 'dark night of the soul', life seemed like an impenetrable mystery. Having explored different faiths and religious disciplines over the years it always seemed that, at their core, they required us to do two things: to believe something because we were told to and to obey the rules in accordance with a predetermined and often outdated set of instructions. There were divine penalties to pay for not following those rules – or sinning – and punishment was meted out from a higher power that demanded both obedience and unconditional love. Whether it be Christianity, Islam, Judaism, Hinduism or Buddhism, there is always a price to pay. When we question the doctrine, often we are told to have faith, or just to do as we are told – to be good, or else! But it's hard, being a human being. We are not simple creatures; we are each one of us an exquisitely complex combination of light and dark, compassion and indifference, confidence and fear – angel and devil! Our journeys are shaped first by our core natures that must adapt to our experiences as we grow up, to our culture and the part of the world we live in and the constant chaos of energy that we must respond to and in which we must create our lives every single day.

Mainstream religion never answered my questions or gave me any clear guidance as to why my own life seemed so unendingly difficult. Nothing really resonated or helped in times of real turmoil or confusion. When I asked why, or what should I do, all I heard was silence.

Tarot changed that for me. By drawing cards in answer to specific questions and, by learning the language of the cards, I was able to find and receive answers.

Jung suggested that when we consult the Tarot the communication we receive is from our own subconscious. The cards are archetypes, images that our subconscious minds understand. And I would agree, but most of us who use Tarot will know it goes much further than that.

Tarot communicates information external to us, about someone else's subconscious mind and physical life. The information that comes back from a reading communicates things we could not know about people we do not know, or about people we do know but would like to understand better. It gives information about the past, present and future and will also, if asked, pass comment on situations, give guidance, offer advice and show where divergent paths might take us, depending on the choices available.

So, unlike other spiritual guidebooks, the Tarot not only gives us a framework by which we can plot a life course, it is also completely interactive; it is the only 'bible' with which we can have an actual conversation. It is completely non-judgemental, and when we ask for advice about a personal matter, what comes back is not generalised, but informed by all the elements at play: the facts of the situation, the feelings of the people involved and the consequences that may arise.

It also doesn't require us to believe in anything, all it asks is that we have an open mind. Everyone must find their own spiritual path, of course, but for those of us who found no resonance or answers in the areas of mainstream religion, Tarot can provide answers and a big-picture overview that can help us make sense of things in a more practical way than a parable might, for example.

The Life Code is about using Tarot as a way of helping you see life from 'above', as a blueprint or an oracle that can help create a better experience. Its philosophy is that success in life is defined by feelings of happiness, fulfilment and abundance, and that happiness is not just emotional but also physical. It tells us that joy is our birthright, and that we create joy by combining specific factors in the right way for the right result – for us!

I believe we can use Tarot to explore life in a deeper way and that The Life Code will allow us to unpack the how and why of every card, explain its relevance and its role in the overall picture of life's journey. Hopefully it will become clear that this is not some theoretical exercise. It is a practical, step by step, instruction manual that breaks down the process of creating a life experience emotionally, creatively, mentally and practically. It shows us what to focus on, how we should regulate ourselves and what we can expect when we get it right – but also when we get it wrong, and what to do about it when we do.

Chapter 4

The Fool's Journey, Redefined

I often refer to Tarot as a book with the journey through the Major Arcana, known as 'the Fool's Journey', the story arc or the plot. It has always appeared to have parallels with the archetypal hero's journey, a universal theme that is often seen as the process of spiritual mastery. When I first started to learn Tarot I struggled to love that difficult Fool's Journey, where we must go through the dreaded lessons of suffering and pain, only to repeat the process again and again, maybe doing it better next time, but always in the name of some pre-ordained spiritual higher purpose. I have always preferred to see it instead of a spiritual quest (although that works, too) as a beautifully described human journey through life. As it takes us from the moment of birth through our early years, learning, experiencing our internal world, meeting our parents, going to school and developing bonds outside the family unit, we then start to experience ourselves in the outside world, finding out about our own will, being alone and how we meet challenges that are painful and difficult to overcome.

This journey in real life (unlike the structure of the hero's journey) is not linear. In real life we don't always figure it out first time and sometimes we feel as if we are just stuck, or going around in a loop. Life is not simple and often the people who are around us and who we are learning from are not giving us the best information. Somehow, we end up having to figure it out and muddle through as best we can, messing up and falling flat on our faces in fine fashion. So, more often than not, we find ourselves doubling back and replaying sections, maybe several times. It's all very confusing.

As I started the process of writing the course for Gayle's client, the word 'matrix' popped into my head. I liked it, it felt good. The title would be 'Talking to the Matrix', I decided, because this was how I saw talking with the Tarot, and that's what I thought I was going to teach. To be honest, I only had a vague idea of what a matrix was (and I love the movie, so…), and I liked the idea of universal energy being the matrix within which this system worked, and that was true; it still is. Ultimately, and rather reluctantly, I parked that title and settled on 'The Life Code', which just seemed to better describe the process and the deck as I saw it.

During the process of writing this part of the book, I could see that a matrix certainly exists in this system, and that matrix is the Major Arcana. The Fool's Journey, when read as if linear, seems to clearly narrate a life experience or, as some see it, the journey to enlightenment. But as I looked into the grid of the twenty Major Arcana cards, laid out in their Realms rather than the narrative line, a matrix emerged.

Throughout the book, I will use the terms 'system' and 'matrix' – 'system' referring to the way the overall approach works and 'matrix' to refer to the framework created by the Major Arcana.

The system describes the mechanism behind the entire creative process that forms our life experience. This isn't metaphorical, a philosophy or an idea – it is a mathematical formula. The matrix works in and of itself, much the same as the grid of times tables works when we first encounter numbers at school. It's a kind of feedback loop. It is the key to the system, a universal law, in just the same way as the times table grid is.

We demonstrate the matrix by laying out the Major Arcana so it forms an ordered rectangular display of energetic functions across two linear axes. This shows us each card's intrinsic meaning, and the effect it has on other cards across each of the lines. Confused? I know, but all will become clear – I promise!

So, in this book, *The Life Code,* the Majors are no longer a stand-alone section with an independent narrative; instead, along with the Royals, they become the method by which we achieve our goal, directly connected to the real focus of our attention — the Minor Arcana, supported by the Majors and the Royals in very specific ways. The Majors separate into energetic groups, each of them commenting directly on and helping with our aspirations within each of the suits. The Royals comment on our personal approach to how we manage each situation as it arises. But first let's start with the most important part of the equation — ourselves!

Chapter 5

The Potential of All Things

Take a leap of faith. You will either land somewhere new or learn to fly. Kandyse McClure

Let's meet our heroes – remember, everything is energetic!

We are familiar with the idea of the Fool leaping into life, taking with him the four gifts that are his to explore and master. Those four gifts are often shown in more traditional decks in a handkerchief knotted to the end of a stick. They are still hidden to the Fool though, and don't inform his decision to jump.

Other versions of the Fool show him simply standing on a cliff not jumping, just deciding whether or not it's a good idea. I decided to show the Fool having made the decision to jump and to see those gifts not carried separately but as energy already within him, perhaps unknown and unexplored but still complete and authentic.

This comes from the premise that we are born complete, our nature already within us and inherent. Who we are at our core is complex. We might have gifts or talents for numbers, science, music, language, art, etc. – there are too many to mention – but whatever they are they come with us, yet to be explored and unpacked, and form the basis of our potential. That potential may or may not be realised. In this way, we can see the Fool's energy reflected in the four Aces of the Minor Arcana. The Aces carry potential but no guarantee of fulfilment. That will depend on how we express those potentials in the context of our surrounding influences: nature versus nurture.

We, as the Fool when we are born, are unaware of our gifts but we have them, nonetheless. I remember learning about 'potential' and 'kinetic' energy in physics at school. Energy is a fascinating concept. It just exists. We can't create it and we can't destroy it — we can only alter it. Potential and kinetic energy are two forms of energy that can be converted into each other. Potential energy can be converted to kinetic energy and vice versa.

Potential energy is stored energy by virtue of its position or the arrangement of its parts. It isn't affected by its environment, it is of itself; it carries all its potential within it. This perfectly describes the Fool right before he jumps. When he does jump, that energy is transmuted into its kinetic form and in Tarot we describe that transformed state as the Magician.

Mastering Energy with the Magician

> *Manifestation is not magic. It's a process of working with natural principles and laws in order to translate energy from one level of reality to another. Manifestation is a process of releasing a potential.* David Spangler

Kinetic energy is the realisation of potential energy, of an object or a system's particles in motion, which has become affected and influenced by its environment. Once the Fool jumps, he is subject to the influence of his surroundings to become the Magician. The Magician must unpack and explore his gifts and react and adapt if he is to survive and thrive. We as 'the Magician' must unpack ourselves, to find out what we have at our disposal and what we're going to do with what we have. We

must decide what life we would like to make with the gifts we have come into this life with. We can see the Magician in kinetic action through the Minor suits in the Two to the Ten cards. This is where we must choose, and those choices power us to the next choice and the next and the next.

The Magician can be seen as the real hero of the Tarot story as the Fool in physical form representing us, in this challenging real life experience we're all having. Too often we see ourselves as powerless or at the mercy of life when actually it is quite the opposite. We are in a perpetual dance with the energies surrounding us. It's not a matter of control; it's a way of responding. Our job in getting to know our own gifts and learning to apply them positively in the world sounds simple, but of course in reality it is anything but. But as we learn to make use of this Tarot system as a blueprint for life through the lens of us as the Magician, we can perhaps start to approach our lives from a different perspective. We can see how our experience of life is created by our use of the elements (our own energy) within it. Rather than feeling as if life is something that happens to us, we can, by understanding the process, start to see how we are actively participating in it, and that often we get in our own way. We can learn to dance and move lightly with the energies that surround us rather than fight them and try to control them. Our readings in this context become a microscope through which we examine our current life experience in order to create a better future experience.

Chapter 6

Baking a Rich Cake of Life (with the Minor Arcana)

A recipe has no soul. You as the cook must bring soul to the recipe. Thomas Keller

As I went through the process of creating both The Life Code deck and the related course, my view of the relationship between the Major and Minor parts of the Tarot changed completely. The deck seemed to rearrange until it became obvious that it was, in fact, the Minor Arcana cards, Ace to Ten, that were the real focus – contrary to what we have all believed.

Each of the card's numerological values describes an energetic position or attitude. They give us the 'where you are now, what you are doing and why' aspect of the deck. They describe our aspirational journey. I would stand by the statement that the aspiration of virtually every human on earth is happiness and security. This is what we all want, and in this light six particular cards within the Minor Arcana began to stand out as if in a spotlight. These cards are the Ten of Cups and the Ten of Pentacles, followed by the four Aces: Cups, Wands, Swords and Pentacles.

These, for me, are the cards central to the process of creating our life experience. Let me explain why.

Ten of Cups

This card, when you really understand it, is at the root of everything, and it sums up why we do everything we do.

We are used to seeing the Ace of Cups in action at the start of every new relationship. That tiny flash of hope, a picture of what it could be like if it all works out. That picture is the

insight of your Ten of Cups. It is your ideal that is represented by the Ace. It represents that which is authentic, at the heart of us, what makes us feel alive.

But why do I propose the Ten of Cups as being one of the most important cards in the deck? Because it's way more than just a pink fluffy romantic dream. It is the most powerful, most fundamental component of our aspiration. It represents meaning in life, what gives us strength and what powers and motivates us.

That's a big claim, but as humans we can endure almost anything if we love and feel loved, going beyond romance (although it's often a factor) to include deep friendships, families and supportive colleagues and teammates, who can offer a sense of connection that provides us with a bedrock on which to stand. Shared struggles and incredible hardships can create a group dynamic that collectively transcends almost any difficulty. These experiences can foster deep and lasting friendships. The connection felt by an army platoon that supports each other and survives through peril as they relax together in the bar is as valid a Ten of Cups experience as a couple and their children feel when they relax together in their home. It is about bonding and security through connection and trust.

Love as a way of being is also the central theme that runs through almost every major religion or spiritual message. If love and fear represent the dual states of light and dark, and truth and falsehood, then it is with love that we must make our choices in life. Love is the rock on which all of this stands and on which everything is built. If we can live there, then everything else becomes a whole lot easier.

Ten of Pentacles

Built on the foundation of the Ten of Cups, the Ten of Pentacles takes our life experience to its aspirational conclusion. And though the Ace of Pentacles carries the same flash of inspiration, the Ten of Pentacles gives us the potential to have a new, more enriched experience. For example, a new job carries the excitement of a bit more money, or independence, or promotion; every new business idea carries the same. Why? Because we believe it will make us happier, more fulfilled. A new relationship might come up as the Ace of Pentacles as we take our Ten of Cups foundation and expand on it. We are building not just for ourselves but for our future and ultimately as a legacy.

But in the Ten of Pentacles, we are building to create a physical experience that is solid and safe, one that we enjoy and if we've got it right, will include a level of financial abundance and physical comfort, not just for us, but also for our family or clan. There is a feeling of 'coming home' in the Ten of Pentacles, a place of destination. That place will also inform and hand down all we have created to younger generations and extended family. The experience of abundance handed on here, whether positive or negative, will be built on a specific emotional bedrock because, as we have established, the Ten of Pentacles is built on the foundation of the Ten of Cups.

That feeling of success and security is not just ours. It builds the foundations of our family experience over the years to come. Whatever our family experience of happiness, connectedness and abundance has been, we must build and improve on it. What we have learned, we take forward and turn into our own version, and on it goes.

This is the entire point of the Tarot journey — to create a life that makes us happy, a life that sustains us and those around us, a comfortable life that gives us a feeling of some achievement and success. This is what we worked for, this (hopefully) is what we wanted our life to be. If not, then it's back to the drawing board, because Tarot tells us nothing in life is fixed or immutable. You can always make it better.

The entire Tarot system is built on the premise that we are in constant motion, in a constant state of change; that change may be slow and incremental, but it happens, nonetheless. Every point of stabilisation through the Minor Arcana journey will be destabilised in the next card, challenged and reformed. Tens in Tarot are the maximum expression of their suit, but that Ten won't stay constant. It will decay and change, as all things do in this perpetual energetic dance.

So how do we maintain our lives at an optimum level? Having reached the Ten, we go back to the Ace and bring in new energy, new love, inspiration and insight that enriches our experience, nurturing our Ten of Pentacles experience to make an even better, more sustainable, more pleasurable life. This is our 'world' experience and it is of our own creation.

The Aces

The four Aces are the touchstones of what we most want and they each carry an important message. The Aces represent the potential of the pinnacle of each suit. They link back directly to the Fool energy; each one contains everything and nothing because they are, as yet, unrealised.

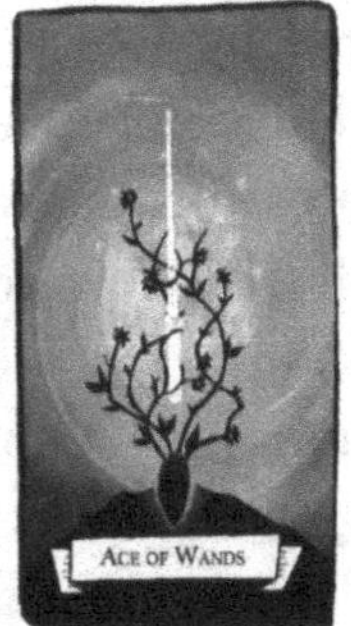

When we observe ourselves at the beginning of any journey, be it a new relationship, job, or our newest most exciting idea, we often have a quick flash, a sudden clear picture of a potential outcome. It is often brief and then disregarded or discarded when confronted by current reality, a situation that doesn't support that ideal. We disregard it because we are busy trying to manage our expectations and adapt ourselves to the present. That vision, though, if uninformed by fear, will give us a picture of why we want this, and that is why, in this system, we don't disregard that flash. Instead, we hold it in front of us like a guiding light, and that's what powers The Life Code approach to Tarot.

Aces represent our direct connection with our higher (spirit) selves, the part of us that receives information intuitively, and it is the Magician that makes things happen energetically by becoming a conduit between the realms of spirit and earth: 'as above, so below'.

The Aces represent that core information from spirit that the Magician can then shape into a reality. The connection the Magician has to the higher realm is through this energetic connection to spirit, represented by the High Priestess card. She represents our internal world — our subconscious depths, our connection to our higher self, both the light and the dark of us and our connection through that to the energetic spiritual realm. She represents the channel by which we receive the information we need, to make the decisions we need to, to get the results we want. The Aces represent what we want, and are gifts of aspirational insight, guiding us towards that ultimate Ten of Pentacles experience.

We build for the future, it's in our DNA to do so, because we believe the process of building will make us happy, fulfilled and, ultimately, secure. We want to be even happier and more secure, so we build more. I teach Pentacles as our life experience, which is our real abundance. Life experience is our currency in life. The suit of Pentacles represents the experience created by combining the other three suits, built on that Ten of Cups imperative. Through this lens, the Ten of Pentacles is the World card. It's our world, the life experience we have created, in our role as the Magician with everything we have at our disposal. But it all comes full circle back to the Ten of Cups foundation.

It all comes back to love.

Tarot tells us the things that we need, in the measures we need them, to make our lives work.

How we reach that Ten of Pentacles experience is through our use of Wands and Swords in the Minor Arcana. These are process suits, our tools. Wands and Swords give us the means to take action, make decisions and deal with problems and moderate our energy with logic and insight.

If we see the Minor suits as layers or components of our overall life experience, we can see how it combines like a recipe. Cups, Wands and Swords are the ingredients; Pentacles is the cake. How rich the cake is depends on the quality of the ingredients we use and our skill in using them. If you try to build a Ten of Pentacles experience without the Ten of Cups at its base, you are missing the vital component. The experience becomes dry, empty and flat. It lacks meaning, which will ultimately be felt. It simply isn't possible to bake the cake without proper measures of Wands and Swords.

Unlike making a cake though, we can't buy our life ingredients, we must make them from scratch. The ingredients we need for this rich cake of life experience are:

1. Happiness and contentment (Cups).
2. Confidence to act and make things happen (Wands).
3. The ability to be able to solve problems, communicate effectively and confront challenges (Swords).

Pentacles is the cake itself, a built, sustainable, abundant life experience with family, clan and legacy.

We have established the Ten of Pentacles is our desired result, built on a solid foundation formed by the Ten of Cups, each at their maximum expression as the Ten of both suits.

In Wands and Swords though, the Ten is not the aspiration. We can find the 'sweet spot' in those suits at the Six, the point where they each come into balance. As ingredients in our cake, too much of either and the results are lopsided. Our cake of life becomes bitter and hard to digest — difficult to swallow.

The Tens of both Wands and Swords are overloaded energies, showing us what happens when we do not use the suits effectively. In the Ten of Wands we are stressed, overloaded and burned out and in the Ten of Swords we are lost in the drama of our minds, feeling like victims, unable to process any information outside our own suffering. Not exactly sweet ingredients to add to the recipe of a happy life, eh? And again, we see that lovely rich cake as a metaphor for the Ten of Pentacles, the culmination of all of the other suits combined and which becomes the aspiration of the entire deck — life mastery itself.

Historically, we have always seen the World card in this position, but I would like to show you how the World card is not the destination; it's an observation about the process.

You'll notice that I haven't yet mentioned the Royals. They work separately, but alongside the Majors, doing a slightly different job again. Their role is to refer to us directly. They tell us in what attitude to show up, and how to manage the different parts of the Ace-to-Ten process. I'll cover their role in more detail soon.

So, as sections, we can see each of the parts of the deck as having these roles:

- The Minor Arcana, Ace to Ten: the overall route to our aspirational destination.
- The Royals: the best attitude for each part of the process.
- The Major Arcana, 0 to 21: the system or rules by which we navigate for the best result.

So what happened to the spiritual aspect of our journey?

Earlier, I wrote about how, when I began studying Tarot, I was taught that the Fool's journey represented 'us' going through a hard yard's spiritual journey towards enlightenment; however, I have learned, during my years of reading Tarot, that something different is actually true. That instead of the Majors representing the lessons the Fool must learn to become enlightened, they become the operational framework that takes us to the 'here-on-earth' life experience that can make us happy.

Returning to the idea of Tarot as a conversation with Spirit, we can start to see their role as guides within that framework as the instruction manual by which each Realm works. We can see the whole process of life as a potential co-creation, with Tarot as an instruction manual from the energetic world and which gives us an overview, a way of seeing how the process of 'doing' life works, how it is constructed from the ground up. It is an enlightened view for sure but the focus is not to do all this to be 'enlightened'. The point is to focus on life itself, our very real and gritty here and now, or as the Taoists might call it, The Way.

This system is there to help us do the work of getting good at life and, eventually, mastering it.

By initially connecting to the Aces via our connection to our intuition, without the shadow of fear as an influence, we will feel energised and passionate about our lives. This raises our energetic vibration and allows us to live at a different level of awareness, out of the dark and shining. The ingredients will have combined perfectly and, in the warmth of the spiritual oven, our life cake rises to becomes light and delicious.

This describes enlightenment in the real sense of the word. This is not just theory or metaphor about some unattainable spiritual quest; this is the real deal, in real life, and it works!

Chapter 7

Using the Suits

To use the matrix, we must always start with the Minor Arcana and the four suits, which describe the way we create our lives – our feelings, our urges, how we think, and the experiences we have from which we learn and build. These four suits are absolutely the centre of everything. Sometimes it's easy to forget just how important they are – more than the broadly theoretical symbols they have become known as. Instead, in reality, they are the layers of us, each layer building on the previous one and which combined make us who we are and how we enjoy (or not) our lives. How we think and feel about a situation will create a desire to act, to do something. Using the matrix of the Tarot as our guide to self-awareness, we can either act or step back from the urge, look at it objectively, and possibly make a different, perhaps better, more informed decision – a choice. What we choose to do will create the basis for our next experience. We will then learn from it, which further shapes and informs our world view, informing further thoughts and feelings moving forward, and so it continues. This process drives our life forward in a specific direction towards a specific destination, thus creating our overall experience.

I was communicating this to a client recently as part of a coaching session. I use Tarot in counselling and coaching as a way of reflecting the truth of each client's situation back to them, to help them to get new perspectives on their situation. In this instance she was apprehensive about how to approach dating, nervous about wrong decisions and taking action that might result in pain or regret.

She wasn't learning Tarot, but as it forms the basis of my coaching toolbox I wanted to illustrate the example of how the four suits represent parts of us and how she could use them to approach decision making.

I took four cards randomly from the top of the deck, one of each suit and laid them out with Cups, Wands and Swords at the base with a Pentacles card above centre — like this:

I had intended to find only four random suit examples, but what I found was a lovely little spread that communicated the point beautifully, and as always the cards themselves had chimed in and conveyed the information perfectly.

King of Cups. This card showed that first she must master her emotional responses, take responsibility for her own feelings and discover what fuels her response to situations. She must be able to detach enough to be able to discern between reactive emotion and core feeling. Then she can decide what her core feeling is, understand what its purpose is, and what's at the root of it.

The Seven of Wands shows her feeling the power of her reactive emotion; she feels a powerful urge to resist going out on dates or events where she might meet new people. Even though she wants to, every part of her defends her position that she cannot. Because emotion is often more reactive than feeling, she must be careful that it doesn't take over or she will find herself defending that emotional rush and acting on the impulse to hide. Wands in Tarot are our fire energy, they are the engine that drives us. They set us in motion and can be hard to control or resist.

The Three of Swords is the pain she is avoiding and the understanding that her resistance comes from hurt from the past that she doesn't want to think about. Choosing to begin dating may well include some kind of discomfort. She must be prepared to experience some of this, though, to expand and grow. The disagreement or argument this card often represents could also be referring to her response to the action to avoid that she is instinctively taking in the Wands section. Her subconscious, by avoiding the situation, is vigorously defending her against potential pain and she may well be having an emotional 'falling out' with herself about what action to take. But if she can look objectively at the situation and her feelings about it, she can decide what is driving her at this moment and what she needs to do to get where she actually want to go. Which, in this case, is a new relationship.

The Six of Pentacles is, as all Sixes in Tarot are, a tipping point. As it is in the suit of Pentacles, it refers to the experience we are creating. On this card we see a boy with a biscuit and a dog who wants the biscuit. We can interpret this as life holding the biscuit and we are the dog, deciding if we want the biscuit enough. The Six gives us a tipping point between phases, between the Five and the Seven. The Five is a backward step, there is no growth here, only a feeling of lack, fear and stagnation, and the Seven is part of an investment process, it's not a destination in itself. It's a step in the right direction, though, where we can apply what we have learned to our overall experience. We will see the result of what we get in what we do next. The question is, though, do we want the biscuit enough to keep going?

With each decision comes a subsequent experience. We learn something from that experience and are tipped forward into the next; whatever decision was made creates the next experience, Perhaps we simply repeat the same experience; it is still a decision, even if made unconsciously, and it still has an effect. It's all about learning and growing and creating a better and better experience as we move through the Seven, Eight and Nine of Pentacles to our aspiration of the Ten.

This, I explained to my client, is how it's done. You can apply this little microcosm to almost any situation where you may feel conflicted or unable to decide what to do.

If we look at the suits with the analogy of a car, then Cups become the fuel, Wands are the engine, Swords are the operating system, the steering, the brake, and the accelerator, with Pentacles being the car itself and our driving experience.

Let's Look Closer

Everything we do is at its core fuelled by Cups. Nothing exists without an internal 'feeling' imperative underneath it. How we feel becomes what we want, what we do and what we think, which in turn becomes what we get. We can see this reflected in the four suits themselves. Cups is how we feel, Wands is what we do, Swords is how we think and Pentacles, therefore, is what we get as a result.

Wands are developmental but are fuelled by Cups — they are the driving force, pure urge created by feeling. It's the emotion at the root of Wands that gives them the passion, drive and desire to create. Wands' creative and sexual energy is founded in Cups, and because they are driven by that emotional fuel they have no means to regulate. They are all urge and passion. When we are following the urge of a highly emotionally charged state, we are not in control; we become unpredictable as the fire heats up. That's why we need the next suit.

Swords are the advanced function. They are the way we steer, regulate with our minds and solve problems. They are often the least popular of the suits; they are, though, if we use them strategically, our best friend. They are the way we control the energy of all that Cups/Wands emotional power. Our minds are constantly trying to figure out our emotions but often get very confused in the process. They are the top line in the process.

The problem is that Swords are deeply uncomfortable with the power of Cups (our emotions), seeing them as nothing but trouble. Their job is to control and steer right? The issue is that every thought comes from within, therefore every thought has some kind of emotional urge inherent within it. This creates a bit of a conflict within itself. Swords are the way we apply logic to that urge so that we can be most effective. Our minds, though, want to do all the work so, in their need to steer the car, they can see themselves as the main event, focussed on perils of the road ahead, disconnected from the other two and that's what causes the Swords suit to be so challenging. The suit of Swords looks like a painful experience, but it's purely a guide to what happens when we let our minds run the show.

Pentacles are the experience of life that we create with the combination of the other three suits. Going back to the metaphor of the other three suits as ingredients, with Pentacles as the cake, how rich our cake is depends on how effectively we combine the other three elements. We can find all three other suits inherent within every single Pentacles card and each suit is a progression towards the experience that the Ten of Pentacles offers as our real-life aspiration of happiness, security and abundance.

Pentacles is not, as it's sometimes seen, just about money. We can better interpret it as the 'currency of life' which is actually experience itself. Experience is our wealth. Our job is to create an abundant, enjoyable life, the richness of which may include financial abundance, but it really refers to whatever makes you feel rich. Also, the more experienced we are, the wealthier we become because we have more to trade. If we lack experience in any area, we become poorer and as a result our 'experience' overall becomes more challenging. The more experience we have at our disposal, the better we are at creating the life we most want and the richer in all ways we therefore become. In the four suits, the cards numbered One (Ace) to Ten give you the real-life stages of mastering each energy, what the challenges are and what we should aspire to for the best result.

The Aces are fundamental in this process. We already know that an Ace in Tarot reading generally refers to a new opportunity, a new potential of some kind, but it's often a little bit vague as to what that opportunity actually refers to. If we see the Aces as the potential of the ideal of the suit, they start to make more sense. Within each Ace, in an instant, we see a glimpse of what we want. We want the best the suit can offer, its sweet spot. This is the point where the energy of the suit delivers its maximum value to us. We can also see the Aces themselves as a progression, with the Ace of Cups as the foundational desire, the Aces of Wands and Swords as the process and the Ace of Pentacles as the ideal destination.

Every time we return to the intuitive flash of potential we saw in the Ace when we first became aware of a new possibility, we help ourselves to stay on track with what we actually want. However fleeting that flash might be, we should see it as a message from our higher selves that something special is possible. Hanging on to that vision is not easy, just as listening to our intuition is not easy, but in reality they are both the same thing. We often disregard valuable information as being unrealistic or because it doesn't fit with our current reality.

Chapter 8

The Major Arcana, the Royals, and the Matrix

The matrix describes a grid that consists of twenty Major Arcana cards divided into four groups, or Energetic Realms. Each card symbolises an archetype representing one of the five universal components of each specific Realm. Every card influences or is connected to not only the subsequent card but also the cards that fall into line beneath it, throughout the other Realms. These archetypes are the components of the process of achieving our desired outcome, both within that particular suit/realm and as part of the larger plan.

So, as we view the matrix from side to side, it will show us the way to navigate each of the four Realms, identified by the suits of Cups, Wands, Swords and Pentacles.

1. The Realm of Emotion
2. The Realm of Energy
3. The Realm of the Mind
4. The Realm of Experience

Each of these Realms has its own aspiration within the Minor Arcana and its own process to achieve that aspiration.

1. The Foundational Ideal: Foundational position to take to achieve the ideal of the suit.
2. The Internal Process: The internal work necessary to achieve that ideal.
3. Regulation: The boundaries and restrictions we must apply to achieve that ideal.

4. External Factors: Factors in our external experience that will influence our actions.
5. The Guiding Principle: The philosophy that guides you through the decision making process.

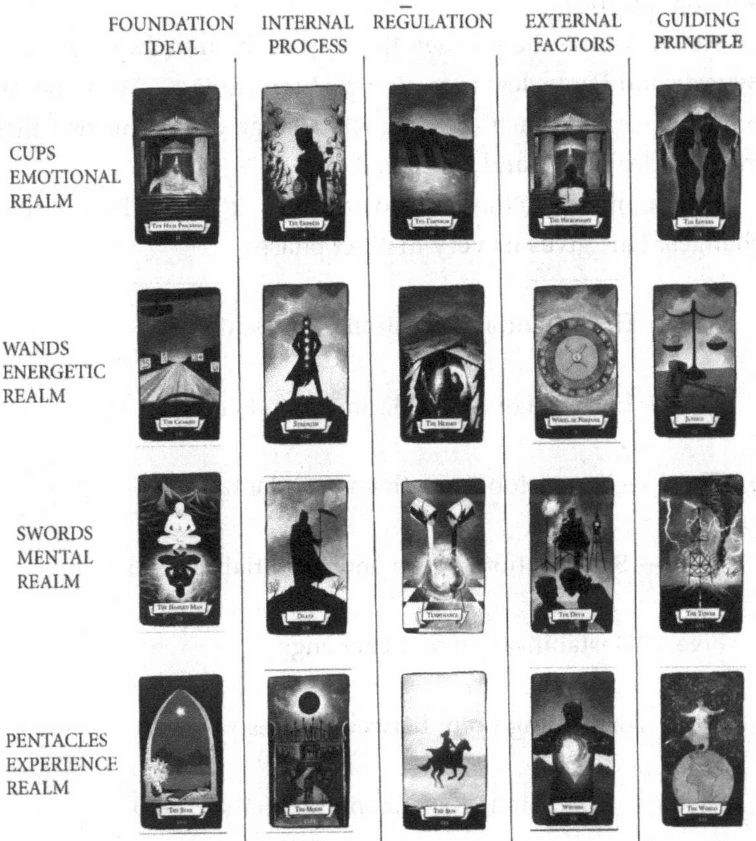

The Role of the Royals

If the Majors give us the rules by which we can best navigate the process of building a Ten of Pentacles experience, the Royals tell us how to approach and manage each phase of the journey, inviting us to embody them through each stage of each suit to make sure we get the best result possible. In this way we know how to 'show up' for the best effect. As each stage becomes increasingly challenging, we are invited to grow subsequently in maturity. You can apply this to any journey or situation you find yourself in and see how this wisdom applies.

As we know, the journey through each suit (Cups, Wands, Swords and Pentacles) is made up of ten cards — Ace (One) to the number Ten. Each card depicts a stage of the journey that must be dealt with and navigated.

The numbers are the same in each suit, it's only the suit that changes. This gives us very distinct phases.

Ace — The potential aspiration of the suit.

Two — Early stage of development and choices.

Three — Expansion, growth and implantation.

Four — Stabilisation, pause and potential plateau.

Five — Destabilisation and challenge.

Six — The tipping point between stages.

Seven — Confusion, assessment; no realistic plan.

Eight — Necessary action.

Nine — Personal experience or satisfaction.

Ten — Connected experience (Maximum).

Each Royal advises and guides through the following stages:

The Pages (the Student) – apply to all Minor Arcana cards Ace, Two and Three – the beginning of a journey, an early stage of development. By embodying the energy of the Page, you are learning about this new situation and you are, as are all Pages, curious about what is possible. The Page energy will enable you to remain open, not to try too hard to control things, but always be mindful of what there is to learn both about the situation and yourself within it.

The Knights (the Action) – apply to all Minor Arcana cards Four and Five – and tell us about the energy required to move things forward. The potential for inertia of the Four and the challenge and destabilisation of the Five can make it difficult to continue in our search for our Ace ideal, and it's easy to get stuck here. This is where we need the Knight energy, fuelled by the ideal of the Ace to keep moving. A degree of idealistic power is required here; this energy allows us to learn to deal with any pain, challenge or disappointment and move beyond it. As the Knight moves towards the Queen though, we are asked to grow in maturity while we keep moving to the next level.

The Queens (the Process) – apply to all Minor Arcana cards Six and Seven – and is a call to bring the ideal of the suit to life within ourselves. We can only manifest what we ourselves are a vibrational match for and this is the time to stop learning and start being. In this way we show up with the ideal energy for success; we must be the example of how it's supposed to be.

The Kings (the Management) – apply to all Minor Arcana cards Eight, Nine and Ten – and is the point where we need to take control. The decisions you make here will affect everyone concerned, but the goal is to stay true to the vision in the Ace and not to accept less than that. Whether we are dealing with the positivity of Cups and Pentacles or the challenge presented by Wands and Swords, this is the advanced end of the process. Difficult decisions need to be taken; experience and maturity will win the day. The King leads by example, he's been through every part of the process and must now take responsibility, making sure things are sustainable not just for himself but for everyone concerned.

Why Does All This Matter?

Understanding the network of connections between the cards and seeing how they form a wider system, each advising and supporting individually and collectively towards our common goals in each Realm, brings a new dimension to how we can understand Tarot as a whole. This system, I believe, shows that Tarot is not only a fascinating tool for the purpose of reading and divination, but it also gives us a view of a much larger overall philosophy of life, a systematised way of looking at the way we see and approach life – emotionally, energetically, mentally and experientially.

A reader who reads for themselves or for clients, informed by this philosophy, cannot help but take on a broader understanding of the human condition and of the spiritual perspective that advises on our struggle to make sense of life and how it works.

For now, let's unpack the columns, moving along the top line of the matrix, and see what roles the Majors play and what functions they perform.

Column One – the Foundational Ideal

The foundational ideal gives you the best energy in which to approach each Realm. It provides the rock on which everything from that point stands.

In the beginning of the Emotional Realm of the Cups, the High Priestess card represents the foundational ideal of self-knowledge, personal authenticity and intuitive connection with the energetic world. In our quest for the Ten of Cups (and ultimately the Ten of Pentacles) experience, understanding our own internal world is ground zero. In order to attract and maintain a happy and connected relationship experience, the ability to be both authentic and self-aware is fundamental.

We must also be able to use and be guided by our intuitive sense to be able to separate 'feeling' from 'emotion'. If we return to the Fool and the Magician, the message is that all you are is already present within you, but you must figure out your own personal components to allow these to develop.

The Magician is a conduit between the physical and non-physical worlds, enabling the edict by which he operates: 'as above – so below'. What manifests in your physical world will be a result of your connection to your internal world and to the energetic world. Therefore, mastery and ownership of yourself are the root of everything in life, the foundational ideal underneath all emotional imperatives (and therefore all journeys). If we go back to the idea of the suit of Cups being the fuel that drives the engine of life, we can also see that the Emotional Realm is also the fuel that powers all the other Realms as well. This makes the High Priestess the standpoint for each of the following foundational ideal cards in the other Realms – all the way to the Star on the final line.

In the **Energetic Realm** we can see how intuition, self-knowledge and authenticity are at the root of the confidence and willpower of the Chariot – the power that enables that passion. That's how we 'know' the right path, and how we are able to commit to it, powering through distractions with single-minded determination.

In the **Mental Realm** our intuitive sense and self-knowledge is also the foundational ideal behind the silence, acceptance, and subsequent new perspective in the Hanged Man. This gives us the confidence and the right kind of energy to stop, let go of our need to control and let life show us a different version, perhaps change our view of things, to trust that we are enough, and will find the answers we need within ourselves.

In the **Experience Realm** the Star represents the foundational ideal on which the Ten of Pentacles experience is built. It represents the ideal of our trust in our own ability to rebuild, replenish ourselves after challenge and turmoil, and faith in our ability to be guided by our higher self or the energetic world. The Star in the final line is the ideal on which all of our life experiences stand. These are the components of our ability to know and trust ourselves and our intuitive sense which enables us to rebuild and re-shape our lives when necessary.

Foundational Ideal to create trust and faith in ourselves:

The High Priestess + the Chariot + the Hanged Man = the Star

Column Two – the Internal Process

The internal process describes what we need to actually do within and for ourselves to enable the process to work successfully.

In the **Emotional Realm** the Empress is the internal system that enables the foundational ideal of authenticity, completeness and self-knowledge in the High Priestess. The Empress card refers to the mother archetype. Its basic premise is that the source of our happiness is internal. Unconditional love, nurturing and happiness within ourselves and who we are at our core creates the subsequent ability to create healthy emotional and physical connections with others.

The Empress is the source of our personal happiness, our passion and all our creativity. She represents the archetypal 'womb' of life, the place from which we are fed and from which we give birth to that which we love, our desires and our aspirations. From this place, we can be constantly replenished and reborn, recreating ourselves in an ever-changing expression of our authentic desire for a life that is fulfilling and joyful. The Empress is the internal system that needs to be in place if we are to make successful emotional relationships and creative choices in life.

In the **Energetic Realm,** the card Strength is the internal system necessary to the Chariot ideal, and it builds from the energy of the Empress to support us internally in times of challenge. The ability to endure discomfort and not be overly reactive comes from our ability to support and nurture ourselves when necessary. This allows us to be more effective, resilient and tenacious, enabling us to stay on track with the bigger-picture goals we want to stay on course with.

In the **Mental Realm** the Death card is the internal system that enables the foundational ideal of the Hanged Man. The ideal in the Mental Realm is that we gain new perspectives in order to grow and be liberated from the constraints of limited thinking. To do this means sacrificing, letting go of our personal directive that things are or must be a certain way, being able to accept and even embrace change. We change the way we think by letting go of what we think we want. For us to be able to do this, we must be able to build on the two previously described cards the Empress and Strength which support us with this difficult process.

In the **Experience Realm** the Moon is the internal system that enables the foundational ideal of trust represented by the Star. Being able to experience and confront our fear is fundamental to our ability to move forward positively in life. Death, as an archetype, represents that which we fear most but, having made peace with the idea of allowing change, we can confront it and any other fear, recognising it for what it is – an illusion. The Moon represents our experience of not being able to see clearly. It also refers to our shadow side, the darkness we fear inside ourselves. Being able to move through and not be afraid of the dark, whether internal or external, is vital to our ability to trust ourselves to be able to recreate our lives effectively.

If we explore the previous three cards – The Empress, Strength and Death – we will see how powerfully they each help us create a strong, foundational internal support system that enables the process of dealing with our fear. Our instinct is often to try to avoid our greatest fears but if we can meet them head on, we find we are liberated from their limitations and are free to recreate whenever we need to, living life at its fullest expression.

Internal system to deal with fear:

The Empress + Strength + Death = the Moon

Column Three – Regulation

The control/rules we need to apply to achieve our ideal outcome.

In the **Emotional Realm** this regulation is represented by the Emperor, in Tarot traditionally the male/father archetype. He brings structure, discipline and rules to the unconditional creative, nurturing well of the Empress. The card gives us a hydro dam, a man-made structure that limits the flow of water to serve a predetermined purpose. It provides a boundary between water and earth (Cups and Pentacles).

Water in Tarot represents emotion and feeling, so the hydro dam is the perfect metaphor for Emperor energy. The boundaries that we decide on, what we will tolerate from others, how much control we decide we have emotionally, are our own. They are not a naturally occurring resource. While the Empress's love is unconditional, the Emperor's love is certainly not. There are very clear conditions and rules attached to the emotional flow here and when applied in a healthy, balanced way those conditions ensure proper balance emotionally. To enforce these boundaries, we must decide how much emotion we are going to allow to flow into our decision making. As the regulating force in the **Emotional Realm**, the Emperor tells us that our emotional happiness is decided by how effective our boundaries are.

The Hermit as the regulation in the **Energetic Realm** ruled by Wands tells us that we must take full responsibility for our own actions. By drawing on the endurance of the previous card,

Strength, the Hermit does not need to comfort himself or to service anyone else's agenda. He is resolute in his decisions to make and live by his own rules. We can see the influence of the Emperor in this process. In order to successfully follow the edict of the Chariot to not be distracted away from that which we have decided to do, the Hermit knows sometimes you have to go it alone.

Temperance as the regulation in the **Mental Realm** tells us that none of this is simple, it is not black and white and extreme thinking won't work. We are looking to use our minds in a balanced way. Not overly reactive, but also able to take action when appropriate. To create the right mix between our minds and our creative and feeling core, we conduct a scientific experiment, testing and examining the results to come to a conclusion about how effective our thinking has been.

Referring back to the Hanged Man, we can step back and observe, allowing life to show us the truth so we can decide what mix of ingredients will make the best 'cake'. Then we can take the next steps in that process.

The Sun as the regulation in the **Experience Realm** gives us the payoff to both the dark fear journey through the Moon and the rather strict and apparently austere process of regulation down through the other three Realms. The Sun tells you that your experience of joy should be the regulating factor of your overall experience. How much joy does this currently and will this (moving forward) bring to my life? As Tarot tells us, true joy is liberation, clear sight and absence of fear. When we know how real joy feels, we can measure all other experiences against it.

Column Four – the External Process

What external factors we will need to navigate through?

The Hierophant is always a complex card. It asks: what do you believe? What were you taught about love and life, what religious and cultural heritage were you raised in? As a result, what do you believe your role is in life, love and society, and what do you believe is your place in the world and life? The answers to these questions form the external factors that shape our emotional decisions.

The Wheel of Fortune refers to the events in life we can't control; we can see it here as a roulette wheel. Your actions spin the wheel and that creates an outcome, then we must walk that path and respond to the results accordingly.

The Devil refers to our temptation to seek external solutions to internal problems. Our urge driven creative fire energy is not easily controllable and carries a risk with it. The very nature of our desire to feel better means that we often attach ourselves to solutions which often, sadly, create more problems than they solve. The Devil card is not about sin or evil, it's about ego and lack of courage resulting in the pursuit of pleasure in the avoidance of pain. The Devil card here is giving us a representation of fake love, a facsimile of the real thing, a movie made to distract and entertain, which is OK except that it doesn't lead to anything real.

Our Ten of Pentacles outcome is built on the real love and connection described in the Ten of Cups foundation. The Devil is what happens when our ego convinces our mind it has control, when in fact the opposite is true.

I have never liked the 'judgement day' image in the RW deck. Together with the title 'Judgement' it suggests the idea of souls being judged on the day of reckoning and although we may know that is not what this card is about, still the image is what it is. Here in the **Experience Realm**, we see clearly in this card (renamed Wisdom) the evidence of the other three suits. Experience has been gained from our practical experience of all of them. With knowledge of Joy in place as the regulation of the experience we want, we can see how the Devil energy was a short-term fake version of Joy. Our physical experience is external and it is our witnessing of that experience that we learn from. From this, we can reassess and choose differently, we learn from doing, and what we experience as a result. Then (hopefully) we gain wisdom. We are the ones who judge and decide what happens next; we can apply good judgement and do things differently next time.

Column Five – Guiding Principles

This will guide us towards our ideal. It's what we must keep in mind the whole time wherever we are in the process.

The choices that the Lovers card presents us with are the guiding principles by which we create the Ten of Pentacles. Choosing love as the north star is not a romantic dream though, it's a complex, difficult, journey. From the call for authenticity of the High Priestess, the endless capacity of love and nurture of the Empress, regulated correctly by the Emperor, and filtered through the belief systems we must navigate in the Hierophant, our decisions about what constitutes real love can be complicated. Still, the message is 'choose what you love'; choose with love.

The Ace of Cups gives us the vision of our version of the Ten of Cups – we must choose what will make us properly happy, so we can build something that lasts; something that will sustain both us and those around us.

The guiding principles of the **Energetic Realm** give us the card Justice, and its message is about consequences. *Take responsibility* is the guiding principle – you will ultimately have to, whether you like it or not. Understand that you will be judged and, as a result, you will judge yourself. On that principle you can decide how to act; what actions to take. Take responsibility for the life you create and your choices (in the Lovers) have meaning and you will have to live with whatever happens as a result of your actions.

The Tower is the guiding principle of the **Mental Realm**. The Tower is the physical experience we have built. We have constructed an identity and a sense of morality. We have put our faith in that and on that rests our security.

When everything hits the deck and all that we have built as our personal construct comes crashing down, though, we have to start again. The previous card, the Devil, warns us about the danger of letting our minds separate us from our energetic guidance, seducing us with the illusion of control. Once that control goes, we don't know what to think.

The guiding principle of the **Mental Realm** is that you can always rebuild, better, stronger, more joyful and more resilient than before, by changing the way you think. It is good that we have been shown the truth; we are forced to re-evaluate and do it better next time, or not, of course, it is always our choice. There is a risk of stored trauma with a Tower experience, but if we can embrace the guidance of the other five cards in this Realm, we will find that there is a way through. It's not easy, but it's worth it.

As the guiding principle in the **Experience Realm**, The World represents our physical experience. Pentacles are of the *earth;* the name of the world in which we live and on which we build. The World tells us that this is 'as good as it gets'. These are the results of your energetic work in physical form. It is referring to your Ten of Pentacles experience. What does the experience mean to you? What does success look like? If we look at the card we can see the Magician on top of the World, feeling triumphant, embodying now the authentic energy that was only potential when he began his journey as the Fool.

Above him are the crowns of the four Kings. Mastery in each of the four suits is your guiding principle. That was the Magician's job; to master himself and his connection to the energetic world so that he could create a world for himself that was of his choosing. That is true abundance and true success. That is the guiding principle of the **Experience Realm**.

Chapter 9

Using the System

Seeing how the cards all relate to each other, forming relationships that I had never seen before, was incredibly interesting. The cards appeared to be working together towards a common aim. The idea that all this was a map of life, the key to the Magician's creative process, was exciting and also made perfect sense – but it was missing something – a way to use it. The theory works, but how do you use it?

I decided to start with the map idea. We have established the destination, the Ten of Cups and then the Ten of Pentacles. What you need to know first if you're going to use a map, though, is what your current position on that map is. It's very difficult to use it without knowing this.

Because the entire process is focussed on the journey through the Ace to Ten Minor Arcana suits, your 'You Are Here' point must also be situated within one of the Minor Arcana suits. With this as a starting point, I decided on an experiment. Choose one Minor Arcana card and then allow the system to create the reading. This gives you what is known as a significator Court card and a primary focus Major.

When approaching readings traditionally, we draw individual cards in answer to an overarching question, assigning them positions within a spread. This process gives us information about different aspects of the question at hand. We could look at each reading as a desire to see what is going on energetically in life; to see what seems hidden to us. By looking at all the relevant aspects, including past and future events, we can then find out how to successfully move through any challenges, in order to achieve the desired outcome. We first accept the principle that at the heart of every question is a desire; we can see within every reading an ultimate aspiration to build towards the Ten of Cups or, ultimately, the Ten of Pentacles. Tarot is working on the assumption that this desire is at the core of everything. As we have previously discussed, these cards represent the Tarot's suggested final destination – an abundant, happy, sustainable, connected life, in which we have achieved what we have set out to achieve.

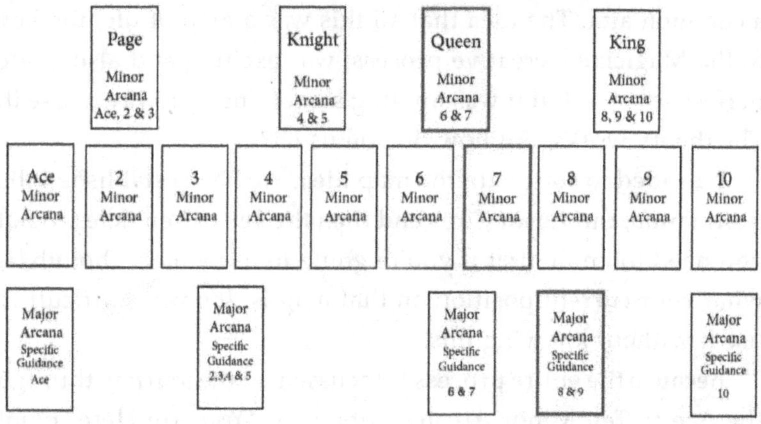

Of course, in reality, big life aspirations are created from smaller steps. Often, we are not looking at the 'big picture', just the matter at hand. But even then, we can see the Minor Arcana process as the route to wherever you are going.

Our one Minor Arcana card tells us in which Realm we are primarily operating (or need to do the most work). It also gives us the current stage of development the situation is currently in. The Six in each suit marks the place where the energy changes. In each suit the early part of the Realm (Ace, Two, Three, Four and Five) is developmental. Beyond the Six it is in a more advanced stage. Marking our position in the Minor Arcana, Ace to Ten progression also tells us what led up to this point, what the next steps are and what we will need to address in order to move forward successfully toward our desired outcome. The Major

Arcana primary focus card tells what process we should focus on to get the best results. The other Majors of the same Realm, laid in order left and right of the primary focus card, give us supporting guidance to stay on track and to move forward into the future.

Each one of the cards is an invitation to consider an aspect of the situation. When you apply them appropriately to the original card, they give you the answer to your question. This part works exactly the same as in a traditional reading, but here we use the structure of Tarot itself to give us the information we need.

This is a really interesting way to do what is in effect a one-card reading. It gives, however, an extraordinary amount of focus and detail around a specific question, by using the connections through the cards to tell the story and while also providing advice.

Card One – using only the Minor Arcana Ace to Ten cards, shuffle and choose one card.

Card Two – your Royal significator. This is the Royal of the same suit that controls the section where your 'You Are Here' card sits. This gives you the energy with which you can best navigate through this phase.

Cards Three and Four – these are the two cards in the Minor Arcana suit that sit to the left of your 'You Are Here' in the Ace to Ten progression.

Cards Five and Six – these are the two cards in the Minor Arcana suit that sit to the right of your 'You Are Here' in the Ace to Ten progression.

Card Seven – this is the Major card in the related Realm that controls the section where your 'You Are Here' card sits. This gives you the process you should focus on to best navigate through this phase. Note what position this card falls into. It tells you whether you should focus on an internal process, regulation, external factors, etc.

Cards Eight and Nine – these two Major cards from the same Realm give you advice about staying successfully on track. What process do they represent?

Cards Ten and Eleven – these two Major cards from the same Realm give you advice about moving forward through the next stage. Again, note the processes as they will be relevant.

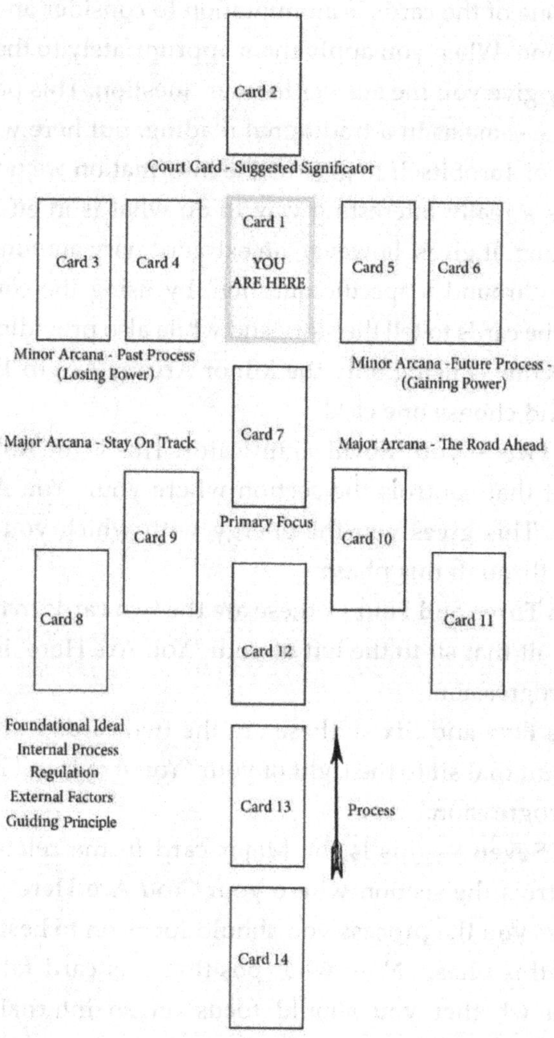

Having explored the reading in theory, let's do a deep dive into each Realm, exploring the whole thing in more detail and seeing how it works in practice.

Chapter 10

The Emotional Realm

Until you make the unconscious conscious, it will direct your life and you'll call it fate. Carl Jung

Ruled by the suit of Cups, the foundational suit in Tarot. They are at the root of all the other suits. They symbolise the element of water, which makes up around 60% of our physical form. Water also covers 71% of the surface of the earth so is, in real terms, fundamental to life as we know it.

In Tarot the suit of Cups represents the same thing, in reference to what is fundamental to life as we know it. That watery 60% is mostly hidden; it's what's inside our constantly moving, mostly hidden emotional and subconscious world. This powerful sea of emotion that is both within and around us is also unpredictable. This unpredictability, in combination with the fact we can't always see what's lurking underneath the water, makes it difficult to navigate. We can go between feeling sublime – like we can take on the world – to feeling that we might get swept away in it and drown, depending on the circumstance or our level of experience. It's that powerful!

Our watery emotional subconscious also works as an energy conductor in the non-physical world, in a similar way to the way water conducts electricity. The more consistently powerful our emotional responses are, the more powerful the vibration into the non-physical world. The resulting resonance is the force that attracts similarly resonant elements into our life and this is, energetically, how we create our life experience.

It is a constant, ongoing dialogue with the energetic world that shifts and changes in answer to our emotional vibration. This describes the connection the Magician has to the energetic world of spirit; it is how he manifests and makes real the Fool's potential energy.

In this Realm, the energy the cards are referring to is shown as blue/pink. The journey through the Minor suit of Cups is a story about our aspirational journey in search of contentment and happiness. Everything begins with a feeling, and the choices we make around how we feel and what or who we do (or don't) love shape our lives in powerful fashion. To find happiness and connection is the most basic of human aspirations and, when we feel its absence, we know life is lacking in a vital and powerful way. Our experience in this Realm and what we decide about love and our core happiness lays the foundation for everything else that follows. If we look at the Emotional Realm as a whole, we can see how the guidance of the Majors and the Royals give us the methodology by which we can achieve our aspirational Ten of Cups objective. They each provide specific advice for each stage of the journey. The Majors and the Royals help by showing up in the process at exactly the right time on the Ace to Ten narrative line, telling what we need to do to move ourselves along and keep progressing positively. While the Majors give us an overall system to use, the Royals show us the blueprint of our own development, the way we can use our energy effectively and take control to become master Magicians of the energetic process.

The Role of the Royals

The Royals refer to our personal progress and show us how we can best use and embody the energy. If we look at the placement of all the cards above, we can see the pattern in this suit as the Royals respond to the changing requirements of the Minors. We are being asked to show up in different ways for different situations. The Royals tell us exactly how to manage the journey through each Realm to make sure we get the best result possible.

The Page (the Student) – Guidance around the Two and Three of Cups.

This is the learning and exploring phase of the process. The Page here asks us to explore specifically what makes us happy. It's easy to overlook this little Page but we do so at our peril. If we don't know what makes us happy, how can we even begin to create a happy life experience? The card shows us a child with a fishing net, paddling in shallow water, watched from behind by a cheeky little fish. The fish symbolises that which lives in your watery emotional world. The card connects you to a more innocent version of yourself, a time when your emotional world was simpler.

This is where we get to know ourselves; remember the directive of the High Priestess, where we figure out our relationship, both to our own internal world and to those around us and to learn to navigate relationships and our need for connection. The Page of Cups is innocent and curious; it represents the childlike part of us. Our connection to our inner child is fundamental to our happiness, the part of us that is pure and untainted by cynicism or fear.

When we find ourselves at the beginning of a new emotional journey, approaching the situation with curiosity and an openness to learn more will bring the best results. How happy is this situation making you and what is your intuition telling you? The Page is a spiritual student, after all.

The Knight (the Action) – Guidance around the Four and Five of Cups.

The Knights tell us about the energy required to move things forward. The inertia of the Four and the disappointment of the Five can make it difficult to continue in our search for contentment and happiness and it's easy to get stuck here. Dealing with feelings of rejection or discontent can bring things to a halt so this is where we need the Knight energy, fuelled by the ideal of the Ace to keep moving in pursuit of the Ten. We must really love the idea of finding our hearts desire and not be prepared to accept less. A degree of idealism is required here, this energy allows us to learn to deal with the pain and move beyond it. As the Knight moves towards the Queen though, we are asked to grow in maturity while we keep moving to the next level.

The Queen (the Process) – Guidance around the Six and Seven of Cups.

The Queen here is a call to learn to tune into and process our feelings effectively. She is also confident in using her intuition to decide what the truth of any current situation might be, not being swept off into flights of fancy or imagination. She asks us to tune into the past reflectively to find the truth about how we really felt and what really happened so we can be guided as to what we really want in the future. She suggests we tune into the High Priestess and be guided by the potential of the Ace. She wants us to intuitively visualise what the potential of the Ace actually feels like. If we can't feel it as a reality, we can't make it happen.

The King (the Management) – Guidance around the Eight and Nine of Cups.

The King is the point where we need to take control. He suggests we need to step back and employ some emotional clarity now because we need to take ownership of the situation. He asks us to take emotional responsibility for our own actions but to look at the situation as a whole. It is time to emotionally disconnect with what didn't work in the past and what isn't working now.

The decisions you make here will affect everyone concerned, but the goal is to stay true to the vision in the Ace and not to accept less than that. That decision takes courage; there is perhaps no clear path available. The King is not leaving for another; this is all him, the journey is his decision. In the Nine we find what we have been looking for, a taste of the real thing; what's important here is that we don't see this in itself as the final destination or become too attached to the pleasure. The Ten of Cups is the energy of the suit at its zenith; we will need emotional maturity and objectivity, understanding and compassion, a degree of personal sacrifice where appropriate, responsibility and creativity in replenishing the energy to manage and navigate it successfully.

Chapter 11

The Role of Emotional Realm Majors

The Majors in each Realm give us the method by which we navigate to our goal of the Ten of Cups. They are the matrix for our experience of core happiness, giving us the words of advice we need to be wise in each situation. If we follow their guidance, we won't go far wrong. Each Major gives us a different perspective on the way to achieve our ideal.

The High Priestess – Foundation/Ideal: Self-knowledge, trust, intuition.

The High Priestess is at the core of the Ace of Cups in the Minor suit. This is the beginning of our emotional and intuitive journey. Our emotional authenticity, before any influence is brought to bear. It contains all our potential inherent within it. As the foundational ideal, it is your foundation stone, a call to know yourself and trust yourself. It tells you that it is *you* who is the core, you are the secret to your own happiness, it's actually all within you. The Ace of Cups which embodies the ideal destination of the Ten of Cups, is made possible by knowing and understanding yourself and honouring yourself and your own intuition.

Our first awareness, from the moment of our birth into life is our internal experience. We are aware that we 'feel' something, we don't understand it, but it's very powerful. Then we gradually become aware that the world inside is uniquely ours. It separates us from everyone else. No one else can see our internal world and we can't see anyone else's. Our internal world holds all our secrets, our aspirations, our fears and our connection to the non-physical world as our intuition. As we previously saw, the Aces themselves are progressional; the Ace of Cups as our core /internal self sits at the root of all other potentials. The High Priestess is therefore also the guiding force beneath each of the Majors that sit with the next three Aces. She is the guiding force behind the Chariot, the new perspective gained by the Hanged Man and the source of hope and trust in both ourselves and a higher power that we call on in the Star.

Her advice refers to our internal world and how we understand ourselves:

- Explore your inner world, meditate, allow yourself to experience what's within to better understand yourself; that way you can know what's right for you.
- Learn to listen to your intuition, you need to be able to trust yourself.
- Honour what is authentic about you as opposed to what's learnt (the Hierophant).
- Understanding your ever-changing fluid internal world is an artform in itself.
- Make space for the light and the dark of you: remember — what you resist, persists!

The Empress – Internal System: Unconditional love, creativity, connection and nurture.

The Empress represents our experience of love and nurture. It's how we learn what it's like to be held by another and to feel safe and connected. Through this, we learn how to bond to another, to be loved and to feel love.

She is the guidance we have around the internal process we need to put in place as we navigate through the journey of the Emotional Realm of Cups. She is especially important though in the foundational *Two, Three, Four and Five* of Cups, as our guidance around our desire for connection with others and our desire to feel good as a result of that connection. She gives us the experience of being accepted unconditionally and our ability to love ourselves in the reflection of that unconditional love.

Physical love, friendships and what feels good are all primary needs. As we explore our relationships and the way they make us feel through the Two and Three of Cups, we find a point in the Four of Cups where we feel unfulfilled and emotionally flat. If we know what it feels like to be loved, to be nurtured and cared for and to be able to nurture ourselves and others in a healthy way, then we will recognise the opposite, or situations which are not authentic or fulfilling for us. The Four of Cups whispers to us and asks us to listen. It tells us that there are always other choices, other opportunities, if we are brave enough to seek them out.

When we have to accept rejection or disappointment, or our relationship experience brings difficulty, sadness or even grief into our lives, as described in the Five of Cups, it is the Empress who guides us back to the concept of nurturing ourselves. She is the source of the love and compassion we must give ourselves while processing difficult emotions. This allows those emotions to be released in a healthy way so we can move on and create something new and better for ourselves.

Our experience of the love and pleasure of the Empress is foundational. If we can't call on our own experience of positive love, it will without doubt cause us difficulty moving forward. The Empress represents the womb — the vessel in which we create life and our wider life experience. She is the source of all of our creativity, the place where the passion and urge expressed through the suit of Cups comes from.

Her advice refers to the way we show up for ourselves, what we do for ourselves, the pleasure we take in life and how creative we are able to be across our lives as a whole.

- Love, honour and have compassion for yourself first and foremost.
- Taking proper care of yourself emotionally and physically is an act of self-love, not an indulgence.
- Compassion for others is your gift to them but not at the expense of your own well-being.
- Honour the creative power you have in your life, to create happiness, pleasure and satisfaction and to be able to support yourself through sadness.
- Life is an abundant, joyous, luscious experience — it's your gift, embrace it all, the ups and the downs; they are all part of the ride!

The Emperor – Regulation: Emotional control, objectivity and effective boundary setting.

This card symbolises the balancing force of the Father. His ideal role provides stability, rules and structure. Those rules give us a sense of security and certainty, they allow us to start making sense of the world and what we can and can't do. His energy, ideally by example, teaches us discipline, objectivity and helps us to step away from our need for comfort. The Father figure

(alongside the motherhood of Empress) provides our bridge into the world. This is the way we learn to manage our emotions and to feel independent and confident. The symbolic Father energy also takes the role of the 'breadwinner', the source of financial support and security for the family unit that underpins our experience of lack or abundance. His expression of love is not so immediately unconditional, we stand in his gaze and he assesses our progress; through this we first learn about the idea of 'respect'.

His approval (or disapproval) and the results of his guidance and wisdom helps us stand in our own power and set our own boundaries. Together the Empress and the Emperor form the emotional foundation of our core identity and how we show up in our relationships with others. We can't do that effectively if we haven't first learned to know ourselves and to love ourselves first.

The Emperor's advice runs through the whole suit but sits specifically above the *Six and Seven of Cups* as the tipping point in the emotional process the suit of Cups leads us through. The Six of Cups is our bridge between the past and the present. Our attachment to the past, whether it be our tendency to dwell in past disappointments or our wish to cling to and relive past moments of happiness again, determines the choices we are making *now*. The Seven of Cups, with its world of fantasy about what might be, what could be or what might happen, must be grounded into some sort of realism or we simply cannot move forward. If we want to reach the Ten of Cups, we must decide to do so.

How we embody the energy of the Emperor will be the deciding factor. The way we apply those boundaries is fundamental to the choices we make in the Lovers card if we want to make real the aspirational destination of the Ten of Cups.

His advice tells us how to set effective boundaries. How and where to draw a line about what's acceptable and what's not. Think of this as the secret sauce in your success on the road to your personal Ten of Cups experience.

- Just because it feels good in the moment, doesn't mean it's OK.
- You can say no and still be loved/lovable.
- Stand by what you know to be right for you, even if someone else disagrees.
- Love doesn't make it OK. If it doesn't feel good, it's not OK!
- Pain, either current or historical, is not an excuse for selfish, bad or abusive behaviour.

The Hierophant – External Systems: Culture, religion, school, society.

The outside world has its own rules and structure and there are all kinds of things we are expected to know and learn. It can be a very confusing place indeed. The things we are 'supposed to know' are laid down by the culture and society in which our Mother and Father live and may build on or challenge their learned understanding of the world, so our immediate response to that will be informed by their position. Religion, school, and society start to shape our belief systems. At this point we learn that sometimes our own emotional response must be modified to comply with the larger view. We must often subdue our own feelings and accept the framework of a system that is not about us personally. We learn about society's rules around the idea of right and wrong and morality, about fitting in, the idea of 'the greater good' and the consequences of not being accepted by those around us.

The Hierophant represents the external influences that tend to come into play through all of the emotional journey of the suit of Cups but especially around the Eight of Cups. It influences our ability to disconnect from that which is not in alignment with our end goal of sustainable happiness and contentment (Ten of Cups). Society's view on how we navigate our relationships and what is considered acceptable, culturally and religiously/spiritually, will play a big part in the decisions we make here. Often, our own belief systems around relationships and what is possible for us are forged in society's view, which sometimes makes walking away difficult. If difficult external circumstances have impacted your self-esteem, then walking away and starting again might seem like an impossible risk – better the devil you know right?

Its advice refers to external factors that you might need to factor into your decision making when navigating the journey to the Ten of Cups.

- Be aware of the influence of your culture and what that represents to you.
- We all play a part in maintaining the status quo.
- Master the rules before you break them.
- Be careful of shortcuts, they are often a disappointing detour back to where you started.
- What you believe to be true becomes your experience.

The Lovers — The Emotional Realm Guiding Principle: Foundational emotional choices.

Its advice as the guiding principle around the entire Emotional Realm is that we are being asked to choose our own path. It is we who choose to accept or not accept relationships that make us unhappy. Who we choose and why is not a random process. The people that show up in our lives will be reflective of our own energy in some way; an energetic match that we ourselves have said yes to.

Every time we say yes to a situation that does not serve our actual desire, we get more of the same. Even if that specific relationship ends, the next will mirror a similar energy in some way. The choices we make around who we choose to be in relationships with are fundamental, so if we are not happy with the results, we must find a way to make different choices.

Throughout the journey through the Emotional Realm we are internalising our experiences. The High Priestess stands with the Ace of Cups as the core of our emotional self. She and it (the Ace) are present from the beginning and with us from that moment on. She is the repository of our inner knowledge, but also files and keeps safe all that we are taught so we have what we need to choose automatically. She is completely herself, she is not connected to another; she is at our core. Her knowledge is not the academic knowledge of facts and figures, this is our arcane knowledge, our knowledge of ourselves and our instinctive responses. Armed with this self-knowledge, we should be able to truly trust ourselves to make brave choices about what we think will make us happy.

The Lovers card represents choices and those choices set the scene, not just about romantic relationships but also friendships and broader life choices. This head or heart choice reflects into our career, how we choose to spend our time and what we think is possible for us.

The Emperor is the secret sauce in this equation; it's what we do with our own will that counts. What do we decide is our bottom line? How much are we prepared to compromise our own happiness or values to the needs or wants of another? How much are we prepared to be a victim of a situation? The question is do we choose short term happiness now by acquiescing and/or people pleasing, or longer term happiness by saying no and choosing a different, seemingly tougher, path?

The Lovers card in Tarot is often seen as the big romantic card, but it's much more fundamental than that. Whatever our emotional ground might be, the desire for contentment and happiness is universal. We must keep that potential of the Ace as the guiding star which makes the aspiration of the Ten of Cups all-encompassing. What we choose as our personal version of the Ten of Cups is a choice we all must make, but whatever our version of complete contentment and happiness is, that choice will stand as the aspirational foundation stone on our life's journey.

This is the advice of the Lovers card. If the results of our choices fall short, we feel that lack as a constant murmur in the background; we feel discontented. The question is 'why did you make the choices you did?' But if we can get those choices right, then we feel calmer, more centred and everything in life starts to make a lot more sense.

If we look at the Ace as our emotional authenticity, before any influence from parents, school or culture is brought to bear, then the Ten is the realisation of that authenticity in combination with our emotional environment. The combination of our nature and our nurture working in perfect harmony lays the ground for the rest of our life experience.

The advice of the Lovers is:

- Choose the path that requires courage and integrity.
- Don't choose now what you might regret later.
- Who we choose to share our time/energy with now, will shape our long term experience.
- Is this *really* what you want — in real life?
- Does this make you happy — really?

Chapter 12

Putting It All Together in the Emotional Realm

Let's look at the journey through the Minor Arcana suit of Cups from the perspective of a new potential relationship that we are keen to explore. The system provides guidance and a foundation to approach each step of the journey without needing to do a specific spread. Using the cards in this way we can use this system as a guiding philosophy.

Stage One – Learning and Exploring

Here you are showing up as the Page (the emotional student) – always referring back to the advice of your team – the High Priestess, the Empress, the Emperor, the Hierophant and the Lovers.

Your **Ace of Cups** is a new potential relationship, it carries within it your desire for something special, a heart connection, the real deal, a relationship that will last and make you happy. The aspiration is not just for 'a relationship'; that's far too broad and puts the other person squarely in control of progress. What does the Ace mean to you, what is that glimpse you saw when your heart decided to give this a try? Check in on what your aspiration actually is. What kind of relationship do you really want? How would that wonderful relationship feel and what would that bring to your life?

Tune into the feeling itself. Don't use words like 'normal' or 'stable'. Even if that might be how you describe what you are looking for to yourself, energetically those phrases mean nothing. Go with terms like easy, natural, connected and happy. Be prepared to use your High Priestess, *aka* your intuition, and not just see what you want to see, whitewashing over what doesn't fit.

What *is* the actual potential of this relationship? Your job is to find out, and you won't know until you actually experience it in real life!

If your new relationship possibility doesn't move beyond texts, emails and/or phone calls, it is still in the Realm of the Ace and not in the Realm of reality.

Two of Cups — This is the first stage of development. The Two of Cups is an emotional trade. It's in the early stages, so hopefully now that should feel exciting and passionate. Stay curious; you are learning about this relationship and yourself at the same time. Can you be authentic and relaxed with this person? Are you looking for the same things? Are you balanced or is one person going faster, pushing things along, or slower, always keeping you waiting for them to be ready? Does it feel natural? Are you confident or a bit insecure under the surface? Be honest about what's causing that. Does what they say balance with what they actually do? What are your instincts telling you? Even if you don't like the answer, don't ignore the feeling. Check in with the advice of your team here, look at the advice of the Empress, the Emperor, the Hierophant and the Lovers to see how that resonates with your experience.

Three of Cups – Expansion. This is the next stage of development. Have you met their friends and/or family? Have they met yours? If not, then hit pause on your expectations for this relationship. How your tribes work together is going to be important; we are each influenced by our own need to fit in with our own friendship group. You are still being guided by the Page here so stay curious. You are still learning about this relationship and must continue to check in and listen to the advice of your team. You must both find a way of integrating into each other's worlds, so does this relationship work with or challenge your respective friendships? It might not be a deal breaker if friends or family aren't on board, but it will cause tensions that might mean uncomfortable choices will have to be made later.

Stage Two – Moving Things Forward

Show up as the Knight (the Action Taker) – continued to be guided by your team.

Four of Cups – As things begin to stabilise, development starts to slow down and often stops for a while. This is where the energy of the Knight is needed. The learning that you did as the Page will have armed you with the knowledge about your own feelings with regard to how this relationship is progressing. This is often the time when one of you may begin to lose interest and perhaps there is a voice telling one of you perhaps things aren't quite as you would like them to be. Check

in with and take one piece of advice from each of your guides: the High Priestess, the Empress, the Emperor, the Hierophant and the Lovers and again be diligent about following that advice.

The energy of the Knight of Cups in this stage is vital to make sure you're on track with your original aspiration contained in the Ace. Follow your heart, but follow the feeling, not the person. If this relationship has stabilised into something lovely, that's great. If it's not giving you what you actually want but is instead turning out to be a constant state of compromise with not enough in return, it will be important to be honest with yourself and the other about how you are feeling. Honour what happens next as being the right step. So often in this position we are reluctant to let go of a situation because we want to make the other person fit our ideal, when actually they don't really.

The Four of Cups is telling us that we shouldn't ignore misgivings by either party at this stage; if either of you are still not happy, you need to be honest about why. How you build or not from here will be important and know that if you choose to 'settle' for a compromise that really doesn't feel right, there will probably be a price to pay later.

Five of Cups – Five in Tarot marks the first difficulty in the first stage of any journey. Here in the Emotional Realm, it refers to disappointment, sadness and regret. No one enjoys feeling this way, it's never welcome but it is a natural part of our emotional life journey. Often our instinct is to try and make it stop, to push it away and reach for something that will make

us feel better. In relationships this can mean the first time the relationship is properly challenged, or perhaps doesn't actually continue at all.

The point is though, don't get stuck here. The Knight of Cups will hopefully power us through the situation in the best way forward. In rows and disagreements it should, by focussing on what you both want, gradually guide you both back to why you're in the relationship and help you both move beyond the difficulty.

In the case of grief and sadness around a relationship ending, the Knight of Cups tells you that while it's important to grieve, it's also important not to give up. I use the phrase 'everything is always perfect', which reminds me that I am always in a process. If something ends, you may have to give up on that situation but you don't have to give up on yourself.

If your Ace ideal is clear, then know that whatever didn't work was because it couldn't work. Ultimately it couldn't have made you happy (even if you wanted it to). Your ideal is not one person, it's a co-created situation that works for both people. Grieve and honour your loss, then keep moving forward powered by the Knight of Cups in search of your bliss.

Stage Three – What's Real and What's Not

Show up as the Queen of Cups (supporting and embodying the process), honour your emotions and get to the truth of them, then follow the advice of the Emperor and draw that proverbial line in the sand.

Six of Cups – Six in Tarot is always a tipping point of some kind and in the suit of Cups it refers to the tipping point between the past and the present/ future. The Queen of Cups sits with her emotional ideal with a direct link to the High Priestess. This is the point where we must move on from the past to the future. There is an idealistic rose-coloured tinge to the Six of Cups, but what is it about the past that is so beguiling? Perhaps a past love is still having an effect on the way you feel now?

Perhaps a childhood dream of a fairytale romance is making a real life relationship difficult? Are you yearning for the way it used to be? Have you been through this before; is it all scarily familiar?

If we show up using the Queen of Cups energy as an approach, perhaps we can tune into the truth of what's really going on inside? What's really needed here is emotional and intuitive confidence to really move forward, if the future is going to stand a chance of aligning with your Ace imperative.

Seven of Cups – This is where we confront the fantasy that we have constructed from our past and our daydreams. The process of really seeing reality and responding to it honestly and usefully is not an easy one. The Queen of Cups again asks you to go inside, check in and really be honest with yourself about the reality of the situation. Seeing a fantasy as a fantasy is a tough call and again checking in with the advice from the Emperor card for a reality check will help this process. What are you dreaming about here? Again, the ideal of the Ace must be grounded in a real life experience, not a potential that never realises.

Stage Four – Making It Real and Owning It

Show up as the King of Cups – Taking emotional responsibility and decision making.

Eight of Cups – People change their minds about how they feel, it happens! It's pretty grim if you're on the receiving end, but in the process of us finding a situation that is emotionally sustainable, sometimes tough decisions need to be made. The Eight of Cups describes an emotional withdrawal from a situation. This is a decision taken with the Emperor's guidance. Whoever is walking away is doing so because they are not happy, not content with the situation they have found themselves in. As the King of Cups we are asked to take the higher emotional perspective and to take responsibility for our own situation; this King

takes the emotional decisions that affect everyone else. There are a lot of questions you could ask yourself as the King here. But the main one is, what is the right and courageous thing to do? We can also ask, what decisions did I/we take that brought us to this point? What could have been done better?

A wise person once told me: 'You can do whatever you want, you must just decide what to leave behind to get it'.

The fantasy world of the Seven of Cups is long gone now and real life has kicked in. Now we have to work out what our next steps are in the real world, with real people. The ideal that we first encountered with the Ace right at the beginning of the process still exists as an aspiration but we're not there yet.

If we use the advice of our team in the emotional matrix and ask the right questions, the answers should be clear.

Nine of Cups

The Nine of Cups is a glimpse of how the real thing feels. A rather delicious experience for sure and it gives us a valuable insight into how it could feel, and perhaps, how it should feel? While this might feel very like the exact thing we have been searching for, perhaps it's not, in reality though, a long-term option.

If it feels so good though, why is it not the Ten? Because Nine in Tarot is very much a solo act. If the Ten is our aspiration, we must include other people and their happiness into the equation. If we are to turn this into the sustainable contentment of the Ten, we will need to call on all our emotional experience, maturity and understanding to manage this situation and turn it into something which does not just serve us alone.

Ten of Cups – The ideal that we saw in the Ace is probably one of togetherness in some capacity. Our own happiness is important but if we are happy alongside others, contributing and receiving in return, that's a much bigger deal. This is not a fairytale, though. With reality (again) showing up as the King we must take responsibility for that Ten, look after it and contribute to it. This is not just about us now. That doesn't mean that the Ten of Cups must always be a 'togetherness' partnership; far from it. But the conscious decisions we make about other people are important in the equation. Our personal Ten of Cups is a reflection of the successful choices we make, with the advice of the Lovers as our guiding principle in alignment with our ideal Ace. This guiding principle means showing up authentically, choosing with love and nurturing yourself and those around you, and taking responsibility for yourself and people you love. Compromise where it's right to do so. Do it properly and play by the rules. Always return to the Ace, keep building and remember, if for some reason it doesn't work out, return to the Ace and start again!

Chapter 13

A Reading for Paige

Paige had been frustrated with her relationship experiences for some time. She had gone through a difficult period of self-examination and healing but had recently come to a better place within herself with the whole thing. She was now feeling quite calm and, while still open to a relationship, was not worried one way or the other. She was quite happy within herself and was aware of this change. She was interested to know what the cards would say, so her question was: 'What do I need to know about my relationship situation?'

Her 'You Are Here' card was the Ten of Cups.

This was lovely and confirmed Paige's feelings of contentment and emotional stability.

Her Royal significator was the King of Cups.

Paige had grown in emotional maturity throughout the process she had gone through, the card supported this. Maintaining this attitude in the next steps of her journey would be important. She was in absolutely the right place to be able to use wise emotional insight about the choices she had made in the past and to understand herself and any prospective partners, moving forward.

Guidance for her primary focus? The Lovers (guiding principle).

The Lovers stands as the guiding principle for making the right choices in relationships, and it was on this guiding principle Paige was being asked to put her attention. When all the other work has been done, we are able to understand and therefore take responsibility for the relationships we decide to have. We are not swept along purely by romance, lust or need. The Lovers asks us to choose with Love (intentional capital), not just for the other person, but also with love for ourselves. We are asked to choose a relationship that elevates and nurtures both parties. A partnership that is made from a heart choice, someone to come home to; the home being inside us. Paige was now ready to make that choice. The King of Cups as her significator told her she was now, and should remain, in charge of herself emotionally. This means that she would also be able to judge, with compassion and understanding, the emotional fitness of any potential partners. This would enable her to make wise choices and also to understand and detach from people who were not in alignment with that powerful guiding principle around relationships that the Lovers gives us.

Expanding the Reading

As we can see from the above spread, Paige has come through a transformative process.

Past and Future: As we track back to the present through the Eight and Nine of Cups, Paige recounts the moment when she decided that she absolutely needed to make different choices. Emotionally detaching from her first serious ex-boyfriend, she then found another relationship that initially felt positive and ticked a lot of boxes, but it ultimately became apparent that this was still not the long-term relationship she actually wanted.

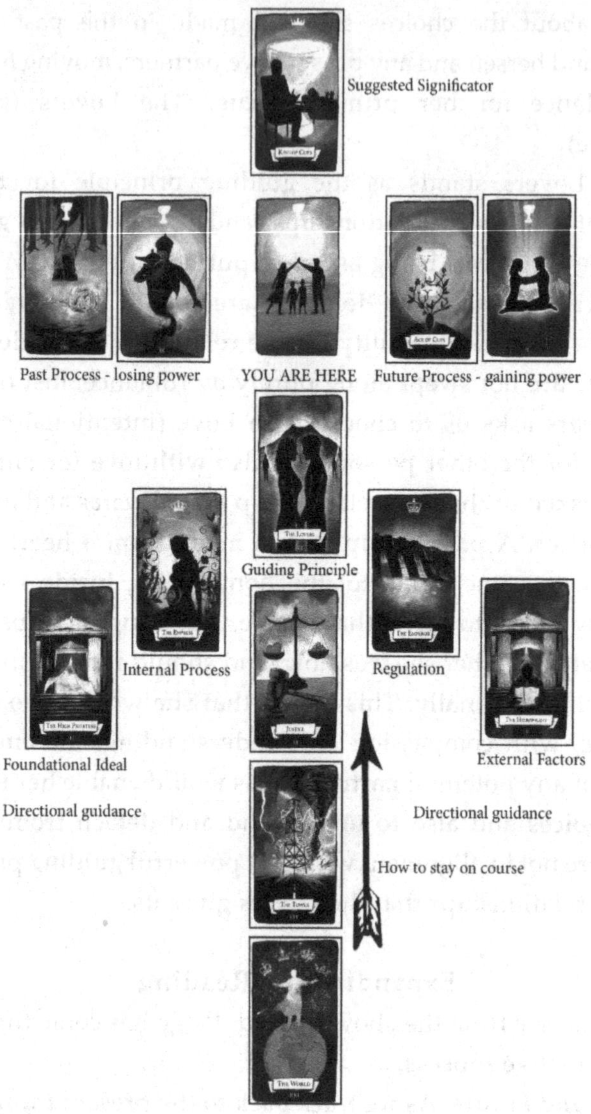

Paige decided she wanted to be happy and decided to be just that. The lovely news was, that next in the process would be the new emotional beginning of the Ace, with a new relationship to explore. Armed with her clear picture of what the Ten of Cups looked like for her, the next card, the Two of Cups would, of course, present Paige with another relationship choice, which led her neatly on to the advice of the Lovers card.

The Lovers, as Paige's primary focus, is supported by the other Majors in the Emotional Realm.

Guidance to stay on track: We can see how the High Priestess and the Empress support both her intuitive sense of what is right and authentic for her and her ability to love and nurture herself, whatever happens. The Empress connects with what feels good, but it's also balanced on the other side of the rod by discipline of the Emperor.

Guidance for the road ahead: The Emperor is the regulator of the Emotional Realm. How effectively we set boundaries and decide on our own limits will be crucial. Then we also have the Hierophant as external influencing factors, looking at what belief systems are in place about culture and tradition. The Hierophant can also comment on the need to fit in with the beliefs of others, so family and existing friendships may either support or challenge relationships in development.

Finally the rod gives us the process by which the Lovers card itself is constructed.

Justice: Taking responsibility for one's own choices and deciding what is right and wrong is at the root of the Lovers card. Do the right thing, make the hard choice and choose with love. The Lovers card traditionally has been a card of choice and morality since the Tarot Marseilles.

The Tower: The shock that comes from a realisation of the truth and the need to re-build from the ground up is often at the root of a major re-think around relationships and choices that have been previously made. Building our Ten of Pentacles ending will be impossible if the foundations are not right. The choices we make in relationships are not simple so we must choose carefully, because if we get them wrong, everything built on top can come tumbling down in spectacular fashion.

The World: Knowing what a successful conclusion looks like is actually Ground Zero in deciding on your love choices. Too often we try and fit ourselves into someone else's agenda, giving up on our own vision of how things could be. Knowing that everything you try and build after the fact, will rest on the relationship choices you make now, suddenly brings 'the World' into sharper focus. The World card stands for 'as good as it gets' and, energetically, we must decide whether a relationship is 'as good as it gets'. Is this going to make a good world for us to live in? If not, we must find our way back up through the Tower and Justice, back full circle to the Lovers card to make another (hopefully wiser) choice.

By understanding the Lovers card through the microscope of its composite parts, its importance becomes evident. This is not a gentle romantic vision of a fairytale, this is the real-life version, where tough choices and consequences must be considered.

Paige knows what she wants now and is resolute that she will stand by that. Right now she's doing everything right, she's heading in the right direction. Her reading gives her everything she needs to know about staying on track to find the connected, happy secure relationship she is looking for.

Chapter 14

The Energetic Realm

The flame that burns twice as bright burns half as long.
Lao Tzu

Ruled by the Suit of Wands and the Element of Fire

Wands are the developmental suit in Tarot. The suit of Wands is the first part of the process and builds on the emotional directive that Cups have created. The Wands passion, that desire to act, can't exist without an emotional urge at the back of it. Wands represent the engine that powers our motion fuelled by Cups. Together they form the yin and yang of our creative life force, with Cups being the internal and Wands being the external expression of this power. This creativity is not primarily (as is sometimes assumed) the creativity that we associate with the arts, music, writing etc., although of course it can be. At its core, it refers to the creative force of the Magician in action. It is our power to imagine, conceptualise and create our lives to be the way we want them. This is the process of becoming 'self-actualised'; living to our fullest potential and doing all we are capable of in a way that makes us happy and fulfilled.

This section builds on the emotional foundations we learnt in the first Realm. It is here we learn independence, confidence, resilience, how to take action and to make things happen and ultimately, to take responsibility for our own actions.

In the Beginning There Was an Ace

At the start of every Tarot journey is the Ace; a gift, an opportunity for something new to happen. Here in the suit of Wands, the Ace gives us a flash of inspiration, an urge to act, to *do* something. This is the vision of the potential we see at the inception of any new project or idea. We see it, in the moment, as already fully formed and successful. We feel how it will feel when something we have just imagined happens. It's so powerful, the feeling is often both exciting and slightly scary.

That imaginative flash is at the root of what powers us forward in any endeavour. We must remember that Wands are a process, a skill to use, not a destination within themselves. They give us the key to using them successfully and guidance as to the way to master what is a volatile energetic process. The energy at its maximum power at the Ten of Wands is where it all gets overwhelming and exhausting — what we have here is a call for balance as described in the Six of Wands.

So, unlike the journey to the Ten in the suit of Cups, in the suit of Wands we are not looking for the maximum expression of the energy, but rather the point at which we can use the energy of the suit to give us the most creative power. Fire energy is notoriously hard to control, so we must use it with care. The Six of Wands is the tipping point in the Ace to Ten Wands process, where we are in control of that fire energy and so able to use our confidence and our creative power to its best effect. Beyond that, we start to lose control, finding ourselves becoming more and more defensive, needing to find coping strategies to deal with the energetic load we have created.

If we remember Mickey Mouse in the *Fantasia* story of *The Sorcerer's Apprentice,* his overzealous use of his newfound magical abilities creates a situation he ultimately couldn't control; he gets completely overwhelmed and ends up making a bit of a mess of things. This is a perfect example of the journey through the Minor Arcana Energetic Realm. Fire, used skilfully and carefully, transforms our experience of life by giving us the power to change and shape our world. When it gets out of control, though, it becomes a destructive force that can leave us 'burnt out'.

We must keep hold of that inspirational Ace vision, however; it's easy to allow that initial vision to flicker out and leave us in the dark, wondering why we started the thing in the first place.

The Role of the Royals

Let's look at the Royals in the suit of Wands and how they refer to us personally, showing us how we can use and embody that fiery Wands energy effectively. Once again, we can see how the Royals respond to the changing requirements of the progressional Minors. We are being asked to show up in different ways for different situations. The Royals tell us exactly how to manage the journey through each Realm to make sure we get the best result possible.

The Page (the Student) – Guidance around the Two and Three of Wands

The Page here asks us to explore what excites us. The Page of Wands is sometimes referred to as 'the Spirit of Transformation'. He really is the sorcerer's apprentice and is shown quite literally here 'playing with fire'. He is learning the skill of visualising and imagining what he might make happen. There is always a

bit of risk in the suit of Wands and the skill is learning to assess and deal with that risk at the first stages of bringing that Ace vision to life. The key is excitement! Wands are born of fire, passion and energy. We need that passion and excitement to overcome the element of risk that always comes hand in hand with any Wands directive. He sits over the Two and Three of Wands as the imaginary force that enables us to make the initial decisions necessary to get moving.

The Two of Wands is a gateway, a crossroads that requires us to choose where we are going to put our energy, which road we are going to walk down and commit to. The Page asks us to imagine each path and where it might lead. Do we have enough passion to start, to make it real? Once we have chosen our path, we are on our way. The Page needs to keep visualising and building on the vision, staying true to the inspiration he found in his Ace.

The Three of Wands asks us to expand our vision, to look down the path and see what opportunities there might be. We are asked to look beyond our current safe position; there is some risk, both in choosing a path and in leaving our comfort zone to find ways to find the growth opportunities. The Page refers to us learning to manage the risk, to be guided by our passion and our excitement for the project or the journey. The inspiration of the Ace must light the way through. The clearer our vision the more chance we have of bringing it to life.

The Knight (the Action) – Guidance around the Four and Five of Wands

The Knights tell us about the energy required to move things forward. The Four of Wands brings with it a feeling of satisfaction. It's a milestone of some kind, the first stage of stabilisation. There is always a pause that accompanies the Four and with that pause, some energy is always lost. It's not a bad thing within itself, it's a point of recalibration, like getting to the base camp of Everest. The journey here has not been inconsiderable. However, there is the need, if we are to reach the summit, not to stay too long. This is where we need the Knight's energy.

The Knight of Wands is fuelled by passion; there is some pent-up desire in the Page, to make his vision real and that desire is being fully expressed here in the Knight as a force of nature. The Knight of Wands provides a burst of energy that pushes through the temptation to settle in the Four of Wands and the challenges that are presented in the Five of Wands. If we can't be tenacious enough to stand our ground in the face of challenge then probably our Ace vision is either not strong enough or we are not confident enough to be able to push through objections or obstacles. The Knight's energy is not in itself sustainable though – think of it as a turbo boost to be used when necessary. We must be able to manage that energy effectively to be able to maintain progress, or we may well burn out.

The Queen (the Process) — Guidance around the Six and Seven of Wands

The Queen of Wands is like a coming-of-age, energetically. She is the embodiment of confidence, and it shines out of her like a beacon. We discussed previously how the suit of Cups is the fuel that drives the engine that is the suit of Wands. So as the Queen of Cups knows and understands herself intimately, having gone to her emotional core and become one with it, she has as a result also learned to use her intuition well. The Queen of Wands takes this to the next level, she takes that intuitive self-understanding and puts it to work. She is absolutely authentic, having very little interest in what others may think of her. She is emotionally clued up, warm, attractive, and charismatic because of that balanced emotional centre. She's no shrinking violet though, this is fire energy, remember, and she will use it if she must. However, she is the key to balance in the suit of Wands.

Her confidence and charisma are intrinsic, not as incendiary as that turbo-boosted Knight. She lives it, she *is* it. The Six of Wands is the pinnacle of Wands energy, where the vision of the Ace is realised. The Queen embodies that Six of Wands success by becoming the definition of Wands confidence — it is her that brings it all to life.

The Seven of Wands is a personal test; the sweet spot of the Six is not a safe haven, everything in Tarot moves and the Six will always inevitably tip into the Seven. As the Queen, though, there is enough personal tenacity to keep going and stand her ground when she has to. She must maintain the inspiration of the Ace as her vision to keep herself on track, bringing everyone on board as the source of inspiration that carries things forward.

The King (Managing it) – Guidance around the Eight, Nine and Ten of Wands

The King is the point where we need to take control. In the journey through the suit of Wands, as we reach the point of the Eight and Nine, things start to have a life of their own. Fire is a tough thing to control and it's just too hot for one person to handle. The King, therefore, expands on the personal embodiment of the Queen and becomes the managing leader of all concerned, controlling the situation beyond ourselves to all involved in it. Wands energy gets quickly out of control and we can just as easily become victims of our own success. The King energy is a step away from the personal, and it's where we start telling, not asking.

The King of Wands is a dynamic and creative leader and we need innovative thinking in times of stress. He provides big picture vision and the process by which the situation can be brought back into balance. In Wands (and also Swords as we will see) the King stands as the way to handle the problems that will definitely arise sooner or later, as Wands energy tips into potential overload. Part of life is dealing with difficulty, and we never get it right all time. Wands energy is hard to balance, all that enthusiasm and energy builds to have a life of its own.

The Eight of Wands is exactly that state. The King must recognise the signs and start to manage effectively. The Nine of Wands in Tarot is the definition of resilience; we might be feeling 'punch drunk' at this stage but if we're going to play the Wands fire game, we will need resilience. The stakes are so much higher now than at the beginning of the process, and the King must take decisions that allow the creative process to continue effectively; these decisions affecting not just him, but everyone around him. The Ten in this suit is the destination to avoid, where things are not working properly. The energy has become too much, but it's a reality and, sooner or later, we will all experience it. We must be able to step into an objective role to be able to find creative solutions to either avoid or deal with what is causing the problem.

Chapter 15

The Role of Energetic Realm Majors

The Matrix of Confidence and Success

The Majors in each Realm give us the method by which we navigate to our goal of a successful outcome. They are the matrix for achieving the confidence we need to make things happen. They give us the words of advice we need to be wise and to get the best outcome when approaching new ideas, projects or aspirations. If we follow their guidance, we won't go far wrong. Each Major gives us a different perspective on the way to achieve our ideal.

- The Foundational Ideal – the rock on which we stand and from which we navigate towards our goal.
- The Internal Process – what we actually need to do within and for ourselves to achieve that goal.
- Regulation – the way we set the rules we need, both for ourselves and around external influences to successfully achieve our outcome.
- The External Regulation – what will influence and exert control over us externally on the route to our goal.
- Guiding Principle – This is the North Star that helps us steer our path to a successful outcome.

Foundational Ideal – the Chariot

Sitting at the point of the Ace of Wands in the Minor suit, the Chariot is an expression of passion, will, courage and determination in response to the inspirational urge to fulfil the potential of the Ace. As the foundational ideal, it represents the ideal energy we need to make that Ace potential of a successful outcome a reality. We will need to set goals, focus our energy,

avoid all distractions and apply our will and courage to the situation to get to where we want to go.

The spark that the Ace of Wands creates is often especially fleeting; a flash, a sudden visualisation that gives us a glimpse of the things we want to make happen. It's the one that has the most power in the moment. The clearer the picture, the more powerful the urge to make it real — but that flash of inspiration can quickly lose its power if we don't keep our focus on what we want to create. Wands' fire energy represents our passion and confidence and give us the means to take action from an emotional directive.

The Chariot suggests that we harness the power of the Emperor to control any emotional response that will distract or disempower us in pursuit of that goal. This is where we start testing ourselves against the external world, learning about our personal power and our ability to stay the course when we want to realise our Ace vision.

The Chariot gives advice on how to effectively apply personal will and courage to get to where you want to go.

- The Chariot energy contains a 'knowing' that this is the right path. There is no further questioning necessary.
- You must have a clear internal vision, genuine passion and conviction for where you want to head to.
- Success is a journey and you must drive your own bus and plot your own course.

- There will always be distractions and dissenting voices that will pull you off course; how you respond to those distractions is your choice.

Your ability to maintain energy, passion, courage and determination, in pursuit of your desire to bring an aspiration to life, will be the ultimate arbiter of a successful outcome.

Internal Process – Strength

If the Chariot provides the raw power, Strength gives us control. We must be able to bring ourselves back to centre and not be knocked off course by the reactions of others or the world around us. Strength shows us how that same application of will and determination applied internally will help us withstand and tolerate discomfort when necessary, enabling us to regulate our reactions and emotions in response to our external circumstances.

Our internal reserves of power and confidence in ourselves are like a food store in winter. When things don't go our way, feel out of reach, or we experience disapproval or disagreement, we must be able to draw on those reserves to be able to respond in a way that is going to serve us best moving forward. Strength also gives us the process that we need to guide the Chariots' imperative through the initial Two and Three of Wands process. How comfortable we are with the process of pushing ourselves beyond our comfort zone will be important in this phase. The decisions we make here are the decisions that count, they will set the path we are about to take. In order to find the success we are looking for, we must also then be able to look beyond the boundaries that have defined our vision so far.

Strength's advice is around how we respond internally to discomfort:

- Finding meaning in the process of going through difficulty will help us endure the discomfort.
- The 'knowing' that creates the drive towards a goal is also a key factor in developing resilience.
- Controlling the desire to 'react' in the moment gives us more power later.

Regulation – the Hermit

The Hermit in Tarot is the point where we develop our ability to be self-reliant. It is here we make our own rules and start to take real responsibility in our lives. The Hermit is the bridge between our internal world and our life experience. He is the way we show up as the expression of what we really believe is true about life. He is the arbiter of balance.

The Six of Wands is the tipping point in the escalation that inevitably builds from all that passion and confidence. The Hermit suggests we draw on our own wisdom at this point. He tells us that we must take responsibility for what we do and what we build. By being able to find the fine lines between confidence, ego, bravery and recklessness, we can better manage our lives and get a more satisfactory result. He regulates the twin energies of the Chariot and Strength to maintain a power base that builds self-reliance and confidence in our own ability to make good decisions. The Hermit is, in fact, the way we use the combination of *everything* we have learnt so far. From the High Priestess, the Empress, the Emperor, the Hierophant and the choices we made in the Lovers. He puts it all together with the raw power of the Chariot and the restraint of Strength and combines it all into his own version.

He also balances our need for the approval or support from others. Everyone needs some support and being able to ask for or give help when appropriate is vital. Over-reliance on asking for (or giving) help to others, though, will become debilitating and disempowering. No man is an island, but how we express confidence and self-reliance in the world around us will show up in the quality of the life experience we are able to create. He is the key to our success in this tricky-to-master next stage.

The Hermit's advice is about our ability to be self-reliant and independent.

- Ultimately you must be able to draw on your own wisdom and make your own decisions.
- Even if you can't clearly see the path ahead you can always take one more step forward.
- Trusting your own instincts and being prepared to learn from inevitable mistakes will build mastery.
- If you find yourself reflecting on the question 'is this wise?' it probably isn't, so take responsibility if you decide to do it anyway.

External Regulation — the Wheel of Fortune

The Wheel of Fortune refers to the changes that happen around us when we're busy making other plans. Luck is a fickle mistress and sometimes things seem to go our way and sometimes

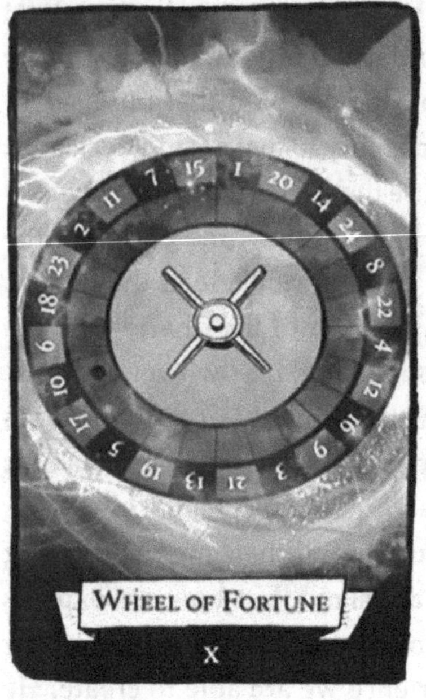

everything seems to be working against us. It tells us that we can't control all of the forces at play around us.

The Wheel is really a test, it's the point at which we get to try out the skills that we, as the Hermit, have put together. How we regulate ourselves in response to how life regulates us will be a vital component in our success as we practise and master our energetic creative power. Life is a continuing dance and sometimes the steps are complicated; as the Wheel turns and we whirl, we must stay flexible and be able to match life step for step, not judging the moves as good or bad, but bringing all our own wisdom, courage, passion and fortitude to the dance to enable life to redirect us as necessary. We can see this in play especially around the Eight and Nine of Wands as things escalate and take on a life of their own. How we manage those situations again will decide the outcome for us, moving forward.

The Wheel of Fortune offers advice about being about to adapt to the capricious energy of life.

- Life is a co-creation; make some room for the 'energy' to make unexpected changes to your plans.
- Our personal preferences don't always make the best decisions.
- By judging a situation as good or bad, we set up responses that ensure we are right either way.

- Fear of change is just a response to the unexpected ending of one movie before you've created the happy ending of the next one.

Guiding Principle – Justice

Justice as a guiding principle tells us to remember we always have a choice, and we need to take responsibility for the choices we make. We will have to face the consequences of those choices in some way; good or bad, we reap what we sow. We can see how the final card in this Realm refers directly to the stress and burnout the Minor Wands potential of the Ten inevitably leads to. What makes Wands energy so hard to control is its inherent unpredictability. The first half of the Wands journey is spent ramping things up, building, creating and moving forward, getting more confident as we go. The second half is spent dealing with what happens when things run away with themselves, or things happen that we didn't expect, or we become reckless, ego-driven or just victims of our own success. Justice reminds us that we must take responsibility. It tells us that the choices we make are our own and whatever the consequences of those choices are, we must own our actions and deal with them.

The Ten of Wands is essentially burnout, a very apt description of the end of the suit of fire. The Chariot has quite literally run out of road and Justice tells us that we need to own, make peace with, and learn from the reasons why. Our ability to take personal responsibility and to be able to effectively manage our own energy and how we show up for those around us and do the right thing will be pivotal in our success.

This is not a perfect or predictable process, we can't expect to get everything right all the time, it's all a learning curve and anyone who dances with that notoriously mercurial Wands energy will experience the overload of the Ten at some point. But we always get more chances, we can always begin again, even if it all went wrong in fine fashion. We can always find new inspiration and try again. Different actions bring different consequences, and so the dance continues!

Justice gives us advice on how to deal with the choices made by us or those around us.

- Everything we do has consequences.
- We are all constantly judged, both by ourselves and by those around us. What the judgement is doesn't matter, it's how we respond to it that has the real consequences.
- Choose to do the 'right thing' – even if others don't agree with your opinion of what the 'right thing' is.
- We may not always get what we deserve in the moment, but we will usually reap what we sow in the longer term.

Putting It All Together in the Energetic Realm

Let's look at the journey through the Minor Arcana suit of Wands from the perspective of a new potential project that we are keen to explore but that we feel we need some guidance on. We can check in on this grid and start asking questions.

The story we're going to tell here is the creation of a new creative business. The Minor Arcana will lead the way, giving up the basic process and the stages we will need to go through. The Royals will advise us as to the energy we can best show up in to make the best of each stage most effectively, and the Majors act as the coaches, standing on the sidelines shouting advice to help us build our expertise and experience so we can achieve our goal.

Chapter 16

Once Upon a Time, There Was a Startup

Your **Ace of Wands** is that flash of inspiration, that fantastic new idea. In this example, we'll explore that idea being a new creative business. It carries within it your desire to create or do something that really excites you. Within this idea is a fully formed picture of the success that will be experienced when this happens. This passion carries with it a powerful imperative to act. You are inspired to action — perhaps you could even say 'all fired up' (see how Wands energy works?). Now that flash might be really quick, and of course, might be followed up by doubt and fear. Put that aside for now and stay with the initial vision.

Stage One — Learning and Exploring

Here you are showing up as the Page (the creative student), always referring back to the advice of your team — the Chariot, Strength, the Hermit, the Wheel of Fortune and Justice.

Two of Wands — This is the first stage of development.

By approaching this first stage as the Page of Wands, we can explore our own reaction to this plan. There's a bit of risk involved here, for sure, but it's an exciting risk. The question you are probably asking right now is, *can I do it?* By using your creative imagination, can you bring that Ace picture to mind and decide whether you are up for the risk? Is it worth it? Will the excitement of potential success outweigh the possibility of failure? You have a choice here. The Two of Wands presents us with a crossroads, so which way will you go? The Chariot is your connection to your Ace vision; if you're going to make this plan work, you're going to have to begin with the end in sight. Again, the Chariot connects back to your intuitive self. Self-knowledge is vitally important if this project is to find the success that its potential suggests. So, calling on all your courage, determination and passion, you decide to go ahead.

Your energetic Major Arcana team of coaches is on board to support you through this process. The Chariot will help with goal-setting and focus; Strength tells you that you can move through any difficulties that you might encounter; the Hermit tells you that you know enough to make the right decisions and can take responsibility for those decisions yourself; the Wheel of Fortune reminds you that you will have to stay mindful of the stuff around you that you can't control, and how you choose to steer through that unpredictable energy will be vital.

The ability to navigate and stay in flow with changing energies, whether they appear synchronous or obstructive, is often the difference between success and disappointment. Justice says that by taking full responsibility for your own actions and being honest with yourself and those around you, you have a good chance of getting the result you want.

Three of Wands – Expansion.

This is the next stage of the development phase. Still approaching this project with the curious, future-focussed energy of the Page of Wands, you've taken the decision to go ahead, so now it's time to commit properly. Making a plan of action is the first priority. Expanding your vision is vital now, doing the research around how you are going to find areas of growth or channels of action to make your project successful. The Three

of Wands asks you to think bigger than before, beyond your current viewpoint, again challenging yourself and any belief limitations that might be in place.

How are you going to take this project into the real world and make it work? Where are you strongest, and in what areas are you not so confident? Pages are constantly learning and aspirational, so this is the stage to really dig in and figure out your route to make this a reality.

Stage Two – Moving Things Forward

Show up as the Knight (the Action taker) – continue to be guided by your team.

Four of Wands – Stabilisation.

As things begin to stabilise, development starts to slow down and things find a point. Here in this start-up project, perhaps there has been a formal launch? Perhaps a product has been created? Perhaps you have reached a milestone of some kind for which you can feel justifiably pleased with yourself? The imaginary world and frisson of risk that the Page moved through is history now. You're in it good and proper. You've made something real happen, and that's pretty awesome.

The trouble is, now comes the hard part. Creativity can be fun in the making; that Ace vision fuels the journey and the only pressure is to keep going and planning and doing it. Once you bring things to a point where it feels like work has been done and there is a sense of completion of the first stage, the next bit can be a tough call. This is where we need that boost of energy from the Knight of Wands. No longer are we fuelled by the imaginative power of the Page, now we need to take things to the next level in reality. Perhaps it's time to take that product/ creation into the real world? The problem is that may well bring you face to face with some difficult truths about how confident and committed you really are.

Coming out of the Four of Wands into the next stage is never easy. It's here, as you move out of that first initial success, that the Ace vision may flicker and fade out of view. There is an element of necessary fantasy in the energy of the Page of Wands; while aware of potential difficulty, he doesn't need to deal with the reality of exactly how it feels in real life.

That's as it should be. Too many projects never get off the ground because of overthinking and the inability to move through imagined difficulties; that's why the excitement and imaginative power of the Page is important in keeping the vision front and centre. There comes a point though when all that stops. The power of the Knight of Wands is like a turbo boost of energy which will power you through the next bit when it might well feel like the energy is not exactly working in your favour.

Once again, those four Majors can coach you through brilliantly at this point as you move into the conflict of the Five.

Five of Wands – Conflict.

Five in Tarot marks the first difficulty in the first stage of any journey. Here in the Energetic Realm, it means challenge and conflict. This conflict may well be personal; feeling conflicted about the way forward now after things went so well in the first

stage can be really debilitating. If we stay with our start-up story, perhaps it's a struggle with marketing – how to do it, or whether it feels tacky? Perhaps there are just lots of obstacles and distractions that now seem to pull you off course? Technology doesn't work, people don't agree or won't help, gatekeepers won't open doors and new opportunities that seemed possible before now look out of reach. Personal confidence takes a hit as you start to feel conflicted about whether this is even right for you anyway.

The energy of the Knight of Wands is important here because it will be the strength of your passion that makes the difference. Following the advice of the five Majors is vital at this point. I would imagine that the energy changes referred to by the Wheel of Fortune are probably playing a part and you will need all your willpower and strength to stay on track. Probably you will feel unsupported and somewhat alone at this point, as the world outside perhaps isn't as interested in your passion or your vision as you'd imagined they would be.

Check in with the Hermit especially. Each of those five Majors has an important point to make in this part of the process, so take them seriously. This process is vital; not everyone will make it through. The Hermit might advise you that it's just not worth the stress. The Wheel is unpredictable, you will have to make these decisions yourself but, if you decide to push through, the experience gained here is fundamental. If done right, it will have the consequence of building valuable experience and incredible confidence, which is after all the pinnacle of our Wands experience.

Being able to move through this difficult stage takes you right to where you need to be — to the tipping point of the Six.

Stage Three — Taking It Forward

Show up as the Queen of Wands to support this project, because your job now is to *be* it, to embody the vision so it can be seen in you. It's *you* that's making this happen, no one else. You are experiencing your Ace vision in a very personal way.

Six of Wands — Victory.

Six in Tarot is always a tipping point of some kind. In the suit of Wands, it refers to the tipping point in our ability to manage our energy and to be at maximum effectiveness in our use of our creative power. Our little start-up business is no longer just a start-up. It's a fully-fledged creative business, having moved through its inception with real decisions made around products and marketing, a proper launch completed with subsequent practical difficulties and the conflicts that always arise, dealt with. Having moved through the mire of conflict in the Five, you can feel genuinely confident in your abilities now. No longer flying by the energetic 'seat of your pants', you are in control of both your own energy and the process.

The energy of the Chariot is proving its worth now, as you know you have amassed the experience necessary to effectively take whatever action needed to deal with whatever life throws at you. The Queen of Wands energy is the perfect underpinning to the confidence and creative vision of the Six of Wands. In this place it's easy to feel unstoppable – and that's great, isn't it?

Seven of Wands – Defiance.

The confidence that we have found in this process is fabulous, and absolutely necessary if you are to build on the success you have already been experiencing. The Queen of Wands is the embodiment of confidence and authenticity. You are the Queen, the face of the brand, with all the vision and passion that go with that clear Ace imperative. That clarity and energy means you are able to be incredibly effective. You are probably getting more done than others think is possible and everything revolves around you, your vision and your inspiration.

The conflicts that may have arisen in the Five are ancient history as you drive on towards new goals and new challenges. This, of course, is challenging, but that's OK, it's nothing you can't handle. Your energetic coaches are standing in the background sagely nodding their heads; you've got this! Perhaps not all of them, though, the Hermit is not quite as convinced. He's advising a bit of caution in how much you can take on single-handed. You can almost hear him whisper, 'is this wise?' as you add yet another project to the calendar. You, however, are absolutely fine with how things are going, because things are going rather well, eh? You confidently defend every decision to expand, you can justify every action convincingly because it makes sense for the project. Of course it's a challenge, but you love a challenge! That's what makes life worth living!

Stage Four — Making It Real and Owning It

Show up as the King of Wands — Taking creative confident responsibility and decision making.

Eight of Wands — Escalation.

Do you remember the warning of The Sorcerer's Apprentice that we talked about earlier in this book? The Eight of Wands' energetic escalation is a natural result of what happens when we play with fire. That sounds like a warning not to play with fire, but it's really not, it's just a fact to be aware of. Fire is hard to control and it takes mastery and experience not to get burned. When we start working with fire energy and get good at it, it takes on a life of its own, things gain momentum, and we can find ourselves going from feeling pretty damn good at getting things going, to playing catch-up as everything we've put in motion builds around us.

If we were to remain as the Queen we would get overwhelmed quite rapidly by that energy but as the King, we now have the experience to step back and manage rather than intensify. We must know where to focus our own energy and what we can delegate to others. The point about The Sorcerer's Apprentice is that it took the Sorcerer himself to step in and take control to get things working effectively. Here in the energy of the Eight of Wands, you can really feel the energetic escalation. Perhaps it's the Wheel in motion? That little start-up creative business has somehow magically grown into something serious. Now we are playing with our feet to the energetic fire, and the responsibility of the whole thing is no small undertaking. Checking back in with the Hermit and Strength, we can make the right creative decisions at the right time so that you don't either become a victim of your own success or your own ego.

Nine of Wands – Resilience.

The Nine of Wands takes us to new territory. All that growth and excitement was amazing but the project has grown and now has a life of its own and that has taken its toll. Here at this stage, you're probably feeling like you've been through a bit of an ordeal.

The Wheel of Fortune is an unstoppable, uncontrollable energetic fact of life, and I'm betting it's changed the wind direction in some way around where you thought you were heading. All bets are off now as to how things might play out moving forward. In every creative endeavour, we must dance that fine line between bold action and risk – all energy work will inevitably go out of balance at some point, it's the nature of things. The King of Wands is a master magician, though he understands the importance of stepping back, finding new creative solutions and organising properly. He's also great at inspiring those around him to ensure the continued success of this endeavour. His vision of the road ahead, through his continued connection to the Chariot, will provide the confidence and drive to keep him and everyone else involved going. Being in control of a difficult process like energy work takes an incredible amount of experience and confidence.

Here in the Nine of Wands, when you're feeling 'on the ropes', rather than the glowing successful vision the Ace promised, you may find yourself feeling more like a survivor than a winner. Suddenly, we can see the consequence of failure looming up ahead and it doesn't feel good at all, because you are going to have to take responsibility for whatever decisions you made through that process. The King of Wands not only manages but leads and inspires, and this is vital if the next step looks like burnout, exhaustion and failure.

Ten of Wands – Overload.

We understand now that Wands energy is a tool, not a life choice. We use Wands energy to make something happen, that's all. When the energy starts to own us and we end up serving it instead, bad things happen. The Ten of Wands is the consequence we are warned about by the Justice card. It is 'all your fault'.

That sounds harsh but the fact is, taking responsibility is part of the Wands deal. Again, sometimes when we play with fire, we get burned, but we don't have to. The Magician in Tarot must learn to master all of his gifts in order to create the life experience he most wants. The stress and burnout of the Ten of Wands is most definitely not part of that picture. There is no inspiration at work here, the card gives us the clear information that this is not fun and really there's no point in it. The King of Wands refers to our ability to draw on and use Wands energy to create changes in the real world; to make things happen. It's not an end in itself – that becomes an ego trip, which can be a problem when getting good at the creative stuff of life. There is an inherent sexuality to Wands energy, it makes us feel good, it turns us on, it excites us, but it can also be addictive and consuming.

Our energetic mentors are there to help us maintain the energy of the King. To return to the balance we experienced in the Six of Wands, understanding that we simply can't always control all elements at play. When we get it wrong, or things don't go to plan; when life swings in a different direction or the wind changes, it's time to return to base and find a new Ace. A new inspirational idea that will either bring things back into balance or, if necessary, light the way to a new path. Because we can always, and must always, be able to create something new and start again with a brilliant new plan.

Chapter 17

A Reading for Oana

The next reading for was for Oana, who was currently going through a confusing period in life. Oana was on a spiritual journey, that had taken her around the world, and she felt guided to come to where she was now, but having followed her intuitive path she found herself feeling as if she was somewhat adrift. She was experiencing the dreaded 'radio silence' that can be so hard to deal with. Oana is one of my Tarot students and so we had been exploring her situation over the last weeks and this spread seemed like it might be interesting to explore.

Question – Oana didn't ask a specific question, she just invited whatever guidance would be offered to her.

Her 'You are Here' card was the Two of Wands.

A Crossroad – choice around a new potential path or in which direction to go.

Her reading looked like this:

Her Royal Significator – the Page of Wands

Curious and future-orientated, the Page is encouraging Oana to find her passion for life again. In order to successfully navigate the Two of Wands, the Page invites her to connect with ideas that feel potentially exciting. They may not feel like certainties right now but that's OK. The idea is to be curious about what's possible.

Guidance for Her Primary Focus – Strength (Internal Process)

A call to be non-reactive to her current circumstances and to be able to endure the discomfort of the current situation. Oana is definitely not happy about how she is feeling at the moment, not reacting to that would seem to be her best course of action. She has clear guidance to stay where she is and stick it out. At this point in time Oana has not found her feet, but there is no sign of a call to abandon ship, instead she is being asked to stay still, to be strong and not react to the discomfort she is currently feeling. It seems to be saying that Oana cannot make the right decision by reacting against her discomfort; there is a decision to be made, for sure, but to do that she must find a way to connect with some kind of passion or excitement about her next move. The right move is not in evidence, so perhaps she simply doesn't have all the information she needs to make her decision right now?

Expanding the Reading

Let's take a look at the cards either side of the Two of Wands to give us some background and what she should do/prepare for next. The process of successfully using creative energy is balanced either side of the Six of Wands. The Two of Wands is right at the beginning of the process to the left of the Six (the tipping point between stages).

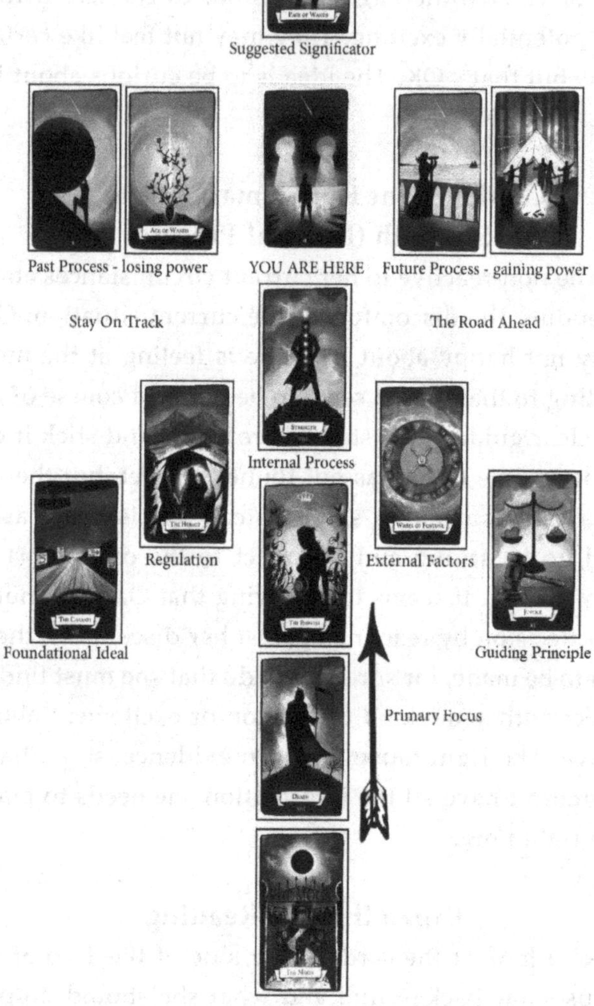

The card before the Two of Wands is the Ace of Wands. Oana has reached this point because she was inspired to be there. If we place the Ten of Wands behind the Ace we can see that she had been feeling burnt out and stressed previously. The Ace was new inspiration, a new potential beginning that could happen in this new environment. She wanted a new way forward and that's the process she is now in. Now she is exactly where she wanted to be, but feels disconnected and vaguely unhappy; she hasn't managed to find emotional connections locally and she has lost the connection to that original spark. She is reconsidering her position; perhaps she should leave and join friends in a different location. She is very definitely at a crossroads – should she stay or should she go?

If we look at the two cards in front of her, we first meet the Three of Wands. This card invites us to expand our vision beyond our current circumstance; where is the growth? What opportunities might be ahead. Remember, the Page is future-focussed, so we are not looking at what is currently available. We might be tempted to read the Three of Wands as a call to look at a different location, the alternative route of moving to be with friends.

We must remember the future focus of the Page though. What would that route mean for the future? Is that a choice that just feels like an escape, or does it offer a genuine path forward. How does that path feel? Is it exciting and slightly challenging? If so, it is worth considering. But what about where she is, this place that she felt inspired to come to? The Three of Wands invites us to explore possibilities that are an expansion of our current position – are there ANY opportunities in the future that would be an exciting proposition? Perhaps a new direction, a way of building from her current position. The route to connect with friends is not new, though. It would be the retracing of a journey made some years ago.

If we look at the next card, we come to the Four of Wands. This is about stabilisation, it's bringing things to a point from which the next stage can be implemented, planting the energy so it can find a home. If we look at the Four of Wands card we can see a Bell Tent, with a warm fire and like-minded people enjoying themselves, a place to pause for a while. Sometimes it talks about quite literally moving house, so perhaps that's where this is heading in the future. For now though, she is being asked to explore and see what's out there.

This is what the reading is telling Oana to be guided by; this is what her inspiration was leading her to. So, if that is the case, might this be her friends in India? If so, why was she not guided to go to India to the Ashram to connect with her friends right away? What potential is in her current location that could fulfil that outcome?

Oana thought for a while and mentioned that she knew a man who owned a retreat centre in the area where she is now living. Right then, it was rented to another tenant but he was thinking of perhaps running it himself in the autumn when the current contract ran out. Oana said she had felt quite excited about the possibilities of becoming more involved in this retreat. She hadn't wanted to focus on it too much because, as yet, that wasn't a reality. I remarked that the Four of Wands card could easily reference a retreat and that perhaps might be something she could explore in future? Again being guided by the Page's future focussed outlook.

Strength, as Oana's primary focus, is supported by the other Majors in the Energetic Realm.

Stay on Track Guidance Is:

To help her stay on track, Oana has **the Chariot,** as the foundational ideal of the Energetic Realm. This gives her a forward-facing card, requiring courage and determination. There is a powerful 'don't look back' message with this card; don't be distracted with other plans, keeping moving in the direction that is in tune with the inspiration of the Ace: 'This is where I need to be'.

She also has **the Hermit** as regulation. Feeling alone is not easy; Oana has not made the friendship connections she hoped she would. She is living alone and spends periods of time not really having meaningful contact with others. She is OK for now, but would not want to continue for too long. The Hermit is a call for us to gain strength and knowledge about ourselves in this time; no-one can help us through this and only Oana can really decide what is right for her.

Guidance for the Road Ahead

The Wheel of Fortune: Referring to external influencing factors, this suggests events around her will change and Oana must be responsive to those changes. The time right now is not right for her next chapter but it won't always be this way. Things will rearrange into a new shape and, if she moves and responds to those shifts positively, her next phase will begin. Oana can't control what others decide, she can't know if the retreat business pivots back to its owner and whether she can find a role for herself. One thing is for sure, things will change and Oana must be ready to change with them.

Justice: How interesting that this potential retreat path revolves around contractual changes. In readings, we often see legal matters represented by the Justice card and it would certainly be a very neat conclusion to see that as the point on which all this rests.

Referring to Justice as the guiding principle as applied to the crossroads presented in the Two of Wands, Oana must make the decision to follow one path or the other. There are consequences attached to both paths: no path is wrong or right, it is down to whatever path we decide to choose. What happens as a result of that choice will play out as different outcomes. We must all become our own judge and jury in our decision making. We must do what we genuinely think is right and then stand by it. Only by doing that can we really find some peace in our position and commit to a course of action. So, the reading has given Oana Strength as being the issue she should focus on. The matrix tells us that this process is an internal one.

Finally, the Rod gives us the process by which the Strength card itself is constructed.

Death: Change and letting go are always front and centre of the Death card. For Oana it perhaps refers to her current situation. She is separated from her husband and is living alone, something she is not used to, so while it was what she wanted and knew was best, it is still an adjustment. To have strength we must be able to withstand the discomfort of change and make whatever internal adjustments we must in that process.

The Empress: The Empress in the Emotional Realm is the well of nurture and love that sustains us in times of difficulty. The Empress energy is a warm hug on a cold day and, emotionally, that's what Oana needs right now. As one of the ingredients for Strength, it tells you to do whatever you can (positively) to feel good, draw on whatever delights you create, and give yourself compassion and understanding. The Empress is no pushover though, she is the culmination of all the Tarot queens so, alongside the emotional self-awareness of the Queen of Cups, the confidence to be herself from the Queen of Wands and the practicality of the Queen of Pentacles, there is a bit of grit in there from the Queen of Swords.

Her strength is drawn from being grounded in purpose, understanding her 'why'. This is not self-indulgence, this is how to get through something tough. You can depend on the Empress, she will defend those she protects and the causes she believes in. She will keep you fed, give you a stern talking to when you need it, and then tuck you up in bed with a mug of hot milk. With her in charge, you can endure almost anything.

The Moon: Not being able to see the route ahead is one of the most unsettling things we as human beings experience. We hate feeling lost, not having a plan or a road to walk down. We tend to fill that blank space with all kinds of horrid stuff. Either we fear nothing will ever change or that we will walk unwittingly into some kind of nightmare. As a component of

Strength we must endure and embrace the 'not being able to see' period. Oana is being asked to experience her apprehension about her future path and the fact that her mood feels lower than she is used to and not lose her nerve. The reading asked her to hold the space, not to react to discomfort. Fear is a big discomfort and while Oana wouldn't describe herself as 'afraid', her apprehension and uncertainty has fear at its root, and it is this experience that she will need to endure if she is to reach that Four of Wands point.

Chapter 18

The Mental Realm

If you think well, you cook well. Ferran Adria

Ruled by the Suit of Swords

Swords are the advanced suit in Tarot. They present an even bigger challenge than Wands to handle effectively. The suit of Swords controls the emotional flood of Cups and cools the fiery imperative of Wands. It represents the way we use our minds to rationalise, meet challenges, problem solve and communicate. Used properly, they are the way we navigate through the 'feeling' to find the most effective solution to the best outcome. The emotional directive created by Cups and Wands can be overwhelming and difficult to resist. We can become lost in the way we feel, unable to find our way, and Swords are there to enable us to cut through this fog and find our way out. As we explore the five cards in the Major Arcana numbered Twelve to Sixteen, we can see these five cards show us the way to use our minds effectively and how to avoid the difficulties we encounter when we get it wrong and let our minds run the show.

We must be able to think objectively and confront situations that we find challenging and difficult. Swords instinctively find both the water-based emotion and fiery passionate urge of the first two suits difficult, they mistrust what they can't control. Problems arise, because Swords have the instinct to try and cut off the emotional flow trying to run the show solo. The goal is to get the balance right, by applying necessary strategic Swords logic and action where appropriate. Trying to work out a mental solution that is fuelled by avoiding the experience of pain as its goal won't work.

The problem is, in doing that, we also cut off from our internal sat nav. When we detach from our emotions in order not to feel, we are actually far less effective. We lose the ability for compassion for others and healing and understanding for ourselves in the moment and can become insensitive, cold and overly harsh. Our intuition becomes impaired in the desire to be right and to take control.

The trouble is that our minds are often more influenced by emotion than we care to think. The need to avoid pain comes from fear which is, at its core, emotional. This makes our use of the Sword even more problematic. That Wands confidence, so necessary in creating new experiences in our lives, can also cause us to wield Swords fearlessly, but recklessly. Building on the fiery engine of Wands as they do, Swords have speed as their instinct and so inherently have no patience. They are ruled by the element of air because this is where they are used. To be effective they must be wielded with some force and intention. Swords must be in motion to be effective but once they are, they are almost impossible to stop. In their desire to get something done or communicate a thought they can often cause wounds that take a long time to heal. Balancing it all is not an easy task.

In the Beginning There Was an Ace

At the start of every Tarot journey is the Ace, a gift, an opportunity for something new to happen. Here in the suit of Swords, the Ace gives us insight, a thought about the fact there *is* a problem. If we view every Ace as an invitation, the Ace of Swords would be an invitation to challenge the way you think about a situation that is causing difficulty or blocking you in some way. It asks us to acknowledge that the problem exists, and the Ace represents that moment where we have the awareness of the problem. In that moment, we instinctively want to move beyond it, to a time and place where the problem doesn't exist.

Nobody *wants* a problem, and often the process of solving the problem feels harder than avoiding it altogether. The suit of Wands and the suit of Swords both describe a process; they are ways to achieve something and, in this suit, we have the desire to transcend our challenge. We find that solution (as we do in Wands), within the balance of how we use this skill; that point of balance is described in the tipping point of the Six. Once again, we must remember Swords are something we use strategically, they are not an aspiration in themselves. The point is to use them only when we need to and in a balanced considered way. Each Sword is a thought, describing the way we think. We can see the Ace as a single thought; one thought about solving a problem. Once we add more thoughts, we become mired in indecision.

The inherent problem with our relationship with the suit of

Swords is that we often see the cards as the representations of various forms of suffering. In a way that's a paradox, because while it's true that Swords refer to difficult territory, what they are describing is our conflict between our desire to solve our problems and our desire to avoid suffering. It's that very desire to avoid emotional pain though, that causes most of the pain experienced in the process. Our Ace in this suit shows a sword emerging upright from the seed, representing the sword of truth and justice. The truth is often concealed in what grows from the seed of the problem, making the solution difficult to see clearly. Here we see that growth tangled around the sword, making it harder to use.

To use the sword effectively, we must cut through the weeds before we can wield the sword in the air to solve the problem. We must get to the truth about the way we are thinking.

The Role of the Royals

The Page (the Student) – Guidance around the Two and Three of Swords

The Page of Swords is historically known as a bit of a spy, and here he can be seen as a teenage hacker finding out information that is hidden to him. He doesn't know how to solve anything right now but he wants to know all the facts so he can work out what action to take. So, when first confronting the problem, we must study both it and ourselves, finding out about our perception of whatever the hidden risk is to us in reality and why this seems so hard.

Again, we must always return to the Ace and the vision of life on the other side of the problem. How does that feel? How would it feel to have solved this thing that is blocking the way? That's the goal, to get to that place. We always have two choices when we acknowledge that we have a problem with something – we can either ignore it, or do something about it, and that is the

dilemma represented by the Two of Swords.

The first task is to work out whether we even want to solve this problem. The Page of Swords is inherently suspicious by nature, he is scanning for where the risks are so, as the Page, we must investigate both ourselves and the problem to work out whether we are prepared to even go there. The Page of Swords is shown hacking into the programs that are doing the processing – what is hidden inside you about the 'thing' and what others might be hiding that could be relevant.

As we move towards the Three of Swords, we now find ourselves needing to deal with a situation that feels challenging and painful. The difficult conflict in the Three of Swords is, at its heart, emotional; the Page here must use the information previously gathered to try and bring facts and some logic to the situation. He stays wary and defensive though, rather than full-on aggressive; there is a problem to solve and it's not easy.

The Ace in the suit of Swords refers to the moment where we understand that a problem exists and that we know that we need to overcome that problem. The clearer our vision of how that solution might work, the more chance we have of bringing it about with the least amount of collateral damage.

The Knight (the Action) – Guidance around the Four and Five of Swords

The Knights tell us about the energy required to move things forward. At first glance, it's hard to marry the 'full steam ahead in battle' Knight of Swords energy with the withdrawal described in the Four of Swords. The Knight (like all Tarot Knights) is on a mission; everything he does is guided by that Ace imperative. In days of yore, Knights would retreat to the chapel and meditate in prayer for divine guidance before riding into battle.

Swords refer to our thinking and our communication with regard to the matter in hand. We need to allow things to calm down, reflect and have time to think to solve our problem after the conflict presented to us in the Three of Swords. That's OK, but if we simply refuse to communicate or engage with active solutions for too long, the situation may become entrenched and stagnant. This is where we find ourselves in the Five of Swords. It refers to the deeply unpleasant 'aftermath of battle' situation that no-one wants to deal with. It's a situation where no positive or emotionally acceptable solution is available. Emotion is not just happiness or sadness, it also speaks of resentment, feeling aggrieved, bitterness or jealousy. Perhaps we might be encountering the aftermath of a fight or a disagreement. Or just what we're left with after a divorce or a broken friendship, or just life not playing fair! A battle has been fought and feelings have been hurt. The memory of that lingers, so the Knight of Swords simply takes action where needed, guided by the Ace imperative to overcome and solve the problem. He's active and fully engaged, putting emotional complications to one side, making sure communication is direct and clear and solutions are implemented with speed and decisiveness. By taking our emotions, our ego and our desire to 'win' out of play, as the fearless Knight, we can take the action which will allow the best, and least negative, outcome.

The Queen (the Process) – Guidance around the Six and Seven of Swords

The Six of Swords is the point of balance, the 'sweet spot' of the suit (if we can use such a phrase when referring to Swords). As we saw in the suit of Wands, we are not aspiring towards the maximum expression of the suit; instead, if we are to solve our problem effectively, we must find a balance, where we can use the suit effectively and not allow it to run the show. The Queen helps us do this by applying the characteristics of the suit to herself as a way of dealing with the presenting problem.

In the Six of Swords, we can see a way forward; the card is often referred to as transition, because it is the process of change, of moving on from a difficult situation to a more positive destination. It is (as in Wands) the aspiration of the entire suit. The point of Six in Tarot is always a tipping point; we must balance decisive affirmative action with cool objective logic, but it's not easy.

The Queen of Swords is the tough love queen – her message is to deal with it and sort yourself out! She is in absolute control, both of herself and her emotions, not letting anyone else's emotions influence her one way or the other. Once action is taken there is no going back; events are now in motion, but we must be able to stay the course and do the 'hard yards'. She gives us the approach we should take within ourselves, if we want to get the job done properly.

The classic Six of Swords image shows us a watery divide between where we are now and the destination beyond. That destination is where our Ace directive lies, but it looks far away and, right now, seems to offer no guarantees. That watery divide symbolises our emotional landscape. The boat separates us from the difficult emotional water and stops us from drowning in that emotion on our journey. The Queen of Swords stays in control to make sure we stay the course. The problem is with the emotional landscape itself, and the lack of speed with which it all happens.

Swords are ruled by the element of air and need speed to be effective. Both Swords and Wands are action-based and find any lack of pace and energy difficult. The trouble is, this Six of Swords process takes time and, more than anything, Swords hate slow processes. Especially if it involves emotions or healing of some kind.

Swords are by instinct quick and clever; they want to think of a quick way to solve the problem with the least amount of emotional processing possible. The Seven of Swords is highly reactive and it refers to our attempt to find a quick fix to a problem, shutting down any uncomfortable emotions in the process – avoidance, distraction, or perhaps an escape. Lies, deception, cheating, concealment, either to ourselves or by others, are all attempts to avoid dealing with something unpleasant and difficult.

We can't waste time raging about what's fair and what's not, we must take whatever steps we can to stop the situation escalating towards that dreaded Ten of Swords outcome. That doesn't mean excusing it, it means taking the drama and emotion out of the situation while you do what you must to move on with as much dignity as the situation allows.

The King (the Management) – Guidance around the Eight and Nine of Swords

The King is the point where, in order to solve this problem, we need to exert control over the larger situation. We are now, in effect, engaged in mental fire-fighting. In the journey through the suit of Swords, as we reach the point of the Eight and Nine, our thinking is out of our control. The Eight of Swords finds us in a prison of our own thoughts, unable to feel or intuit what we should do next. The overthinking that imprisons us during these times is debilitating. Our minds mirror the 'spinning ball of doom' we see when our computer freezes, unable to process the next instruction.

The King here again advises us to step back, we must decide to act, and to do that we must become coldly logical, assessing the situation from the outside not from within. The King makes the decisions that steer the situation away from drama.

Swords energy, like Wands, is bold, but while Wands is powered by passion, Swords is powered by objectivity. Whatever the decision you must make, it will have risks. In the Eight of Swords we are overcome with the wall of potential risk that our minds have created. We must take a decision to move forward somehow and, to do that, the King takes an overview. He chooses the path that is objectively and logically right, whatever the risks are. Letting the evidence lead the way means you can justify your choice and make peace with the outcome. The Nine of Swords is what happens when we don't effectively manage the situation

at the Eight of Swords. The nightmare of the Nine of Swords refers to our fear of the worst case scenario. When our minds are running the show, we become a victim of our thoughts and therefore a victim of life. The King of Swords advises us to step back from our nightmare movie and make the tough decisions necessary. Only using our mind to do what the suit of Swords are designed to do — cut through the tangle, meet challenges, solve problems and communicate clearly.

The suit of Swords does not refer to an inevitable descent into the hell of the Ten, it tells us what to do to avoid it. Swords are the mechanism by which we steer, strategise and problem solve; we only ever need one sword (represented by the Ace). More thoughts (more Swords) lead to more conflict both internally and externally. The King is the master Swordsmith, he is the judge. His decisions are fair and balanced, and he makes one judgement, based on presenting evidence and logic. He is the ultimate master of the mind and he is the way we manage our anxiety, our overthinking and our nightmares. Should all else fail and we find ourselves in the drama and victimhood of the Ten of Swords, we will have to choose ultimately, but to return to the Ace to find the solution that will cut through the noise and lead us back to calm.

Chapter 19

The Role of the Majors and the Matrix of Psychological Success

The Majors in the cold, airborne suit of Swords, show us the process by which we navigate the journey through the Minors in search of the best way to solve problems, gain clarity, insight and the ability to deal with challenges. As we discovered in the suit of Wands, we are not looking for the maximum expression of the energy, we are looking to use the suit of Swords strategically. The point where we can use our mind to its best effect. This is definitely not an aspirational journey to the Ten, again that's where we find it all gets out of control; it is another call for balance at the Six. This is the point where we are effectively able to transition from 'difficult to let go of' negative emotions and find a new outcome. The journey through the Six of Swords is not an easy one, we are often not able to simply dump our problems at will – we can't just fix it. It's a process, it takes time, and as we see as we reach the Seven of Swords, we find the point at which Swords' impatience becomes problematic. The Majors guide us through the process acknowledging the challenges we all face when using our minds in the face of challenge.

The Ideal: the Hanged Man

The Hanged Man as the ideal of the suit of Swords and the Mental Realm gives us the foundation to the entire approach of this difficult Realm. By letting go of our stories and sacrificing our own agenda, we can think differently. We gain a new perspective. The Hanged Man suggests patience (something Swords have trouble with) and it tells us that it could well be our own resistance to change or whatever the current situation is that is causing the problem. This resistance is very evident in the stalemate scenario we encounter in the Two of Swords. In this card we're just avoiding it completely; we literally can't think our way through because the pain we envisage encountering, as a result of engaging with choices we don't want to have to make, feels like too big an ask. But avoiding it won't help. First, we must accept the problem must be solved and sacrifice ourselves and our personal story to the process. The Ace of Swords describes our recognition of, and subsequent desire to, solve a problem we don't want to have. It tells us that if we are to solve that problem, we will need new insight and clarity that cuts through the noise; we will need to think differently. The Hanged Man tells us that if we can just allow ourselves to accept things, stop struggling, stop thinking and allow the process and our intuition to guide us, we will find that new way of seeing things and so be able to solve the problem more effectively. We are being asked first for complete acceptance of a situation, patient

in the knowledge that we will find a way through to the transition offered by the Six of Swords.

Internal System: Death

The Death card represents that painful process of change and transcendence. Acceptance of change and loss is made harder by the emotional pain we experience. It's all internally focussed. As our minds rebel against that pain in the Three of Swords, we make it worse by resisting the feelings, fighting to hang on to what we ultimately must let go. Death is the necessary internal process by which that acceptance happens. We cannot solve problems effectively without being able to let go of something, like a life situation, or our own agenda. As we encounter the Four of Swords, we can find some respite, to allow things to settle and find a new balance between our emotions and our minds.

Regulation: Temperance

Temperance is the 'secret sauce' in this tricky Realm. In order to effectively solve our problem, Temperance advises we must learn to be in control of the balance between our minds and our emotional responses. Not blocking the flow of emotion, but not being absorbed by it either.

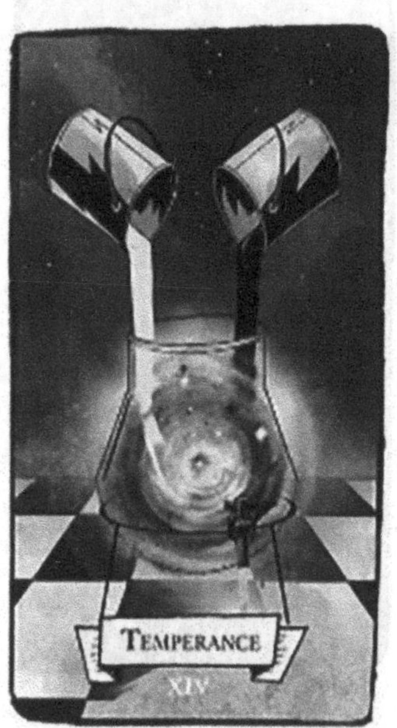

Stepping out of the temptation to see everything as black and white, we can find some balance; acceptance of pain without descending into catastrophe, drama or fear. It reminds us that in order to be able to move on and embrace the process offered to us by the Six of Swords, we can't rush to find a quick solution. Whatever has happened will take its own time to heal and resolve. The Three of Swords presents us with a red heart which tells us that there is a powerful emotional component to the problem. The scene in the Six of Swords, which is the tipping point to moving beyond this difficulty, gives us an ocean to cross, a symbolic watery emotional landscape. The destination, while visible, still looks far away and presents a daunting challenge in its own right. It shows us the journey we need to make to traverse the emotional pain; it's not a quick fix though, and the temptation to try and fix it faster by being clever and bucking the system will ultimately only make things worse.

Temperance guides us to find the right mix, an alchemy of mind and emotion that will support us properly through the current turbulence to a place of calm on the other side.

External System: the Devil

The Devil describes what happens when we reach outside of ourselves to find a quick fix solution that appears to make us feel better. As direct guidance on the Seven of Swords, it tells us that being self-absorbed and focussing on trying to make ourselves feel better in the moment will only result in us digging ourselves in deeper, or creating more problems down the line. Our desire to regain some control or avoid dealing with the problem that we feel is too painful or difficult is a powerful one. We humans hate discomfort and pain and will look for any solution that

will offer either an escape or avoidance of having to deal with a situation that we find unpleasant or challenging.

The Devil also offers guidance around the Eight of Swords. Here we are boxed into a cage made quite literally of our own thoughts. We are trapped, going round and round in our heads, unable to think our way out. We have become hypnotised by difficulty; our thinking is limited to the solutions we have already tried or are too afraid to try.

There is often a call back to the Lovers card here. Remembering that our Ten of Pentacles aspiration is built on a solid foundation of love, we can see here in the Devil card that the vision in front of us is not real, we are not seeing or thinking clearly. A distraction from the real thing. We cannot build a real Ten of Pentacles outcome on fake love; it will never work.

The Devil is not an evil demon that possesses us and then keep us enslaved; it is guidance that simply tells us that it is our own minds that cause the problem, creating 'devils' of our minds by attaching ourselves to solutions which provide relief in the moment but are not in themselves sustainable. As we can see in our descent to the Ten of Swords, we are not nearly as clever as we think we are, and sadly, are often the masters of our own misery.

Guiding Principle: the Tower

We must always be able to accept the truth and rebuild our vision of ourselves. The Tower is offering direct guidance for the final cards in the Swords journey, the Nine and Ten of Swords.

The Tower is mentally a very challenging card. It dismantles what we thought was true and tells us we must begin again. The Nine of Swords is known colloquially as the nightmare card. It describes us living in a personal reality that is probably as close to hell as we can get in real life. All of our fears are ramped up in this very visceral encounter with our shadow. Our anxieties, our insecurities and our dread, all come out to play as our mind plays us a horror movie of our own making. The Ten of Swords is a full-on drama card, where we just fall into the pain, feeling at this point that life is just against us, that we are a victim of circumstance and there's nothing we can do about it. The Tower refers directly to that perspective.

While it's true, sometimes life is challenging, and sometimes, in the eye of the storm, we see no way forward, the Tower tells us that none of that is actually true. We can and must be able to rebuild, and better next time. The Ten of Swords describes our feelings of anger and powerlessness when life doesn't deliver what we thought it would.

The Tower is the point where we come face to face with the truth we simply can't avoid. Life is not always fair, sometimes we fall, fail or things don't work out. Perhaps we are not who we thought we were, or someone else isn't who we thought they were. We are shocked into a new version of reality and we don't like it, but we can and must deal with it. The call for us to develop mental toughness runs through the suit of Swords like a core of steel. The Hanged Man ideal that supports this entire Realm is to let go of our stories, about ourselves and about life. Without drama stories informing our perception, we are better able to make good decisions. Here in the Ten of Swords we can see what happens when our mind runs amok. As a response to that mental meltdown, the Tower is as tough love as it gets; we will be forced to change our thinking whether we like it or not. The challenge now is to transition from feeling like a victim of life to using our minds and our emotions in a more balanced way in order to solve the problems we need to solve. That way, we can rebuild a version of ourselves that can meet challenges head on. From that perspective, we can prevail and actually thrive, with whatever life might deliver.

Chapter 20

Once Upon a Time, There Was a Garden Wall

Your **Ace of Swords** is that flash of insight, the moment we understand that there is a problem to solve and exactly what the problem is. In this little story we'll explore that problem being a dispute about a garden wall that has been rebuilt while you were away, 15 cm over the property boundary. This Ace carries within it your desire not to have this problem; for it to be solved so you can move beyond it. It also carries within it some understanding of the difficulty involved and what must be overcome in the process. The Ace of Swords imperative carries none of the excitement of the Ace of Wands, it is often a moment met by a more grim realisation that there is a challenge ahead that we would rather not face.

Stage One – Learning and Exploring

Here, you are showing up as the Page (the analytical student), always referring back to the advice of your team – the Hanged Man, Death, Temperance, the Devil and the Tower.

Two of Swords – This is the first stage of development.

By approaching this first stage as the Page of Swords, we can explore the facts as we know them so we can make a decision about what action to take. What exactly is going on? Why has this happened? Approaching this project with the investigative energy of the Page of Swords, a conversation was had but it didn't go well. You found the neighbour to be disinterested in your plants and unwilling to take down the wall. Stalemate resulted with no action taken. Your energetic Major Arcana team of coaches are on board to support you through this process. The Hanged Man will help with patience, Death is the realisation that the flowerbed this wall is now on has been spoilt and some of the plants you so carefully nurtured have been destroyed. Temperance advises you not to be hasty or extreme in your reactions; perhaps there is a compromise here that can be found? The Devil warns you about your desire for potential retaliation and the Tower is the shock of the whole thing.

Three of Swords – Expansion.

This is the next stage of the development phase. The Three of Swords takes us to the inevitable falling out between you and the neighbour. You are terribly hurt by his behaviour and the loss of your garden space. Conversations are challenging and combative. You have threatened him with a legal battle but he won't budge.

Stage Two – Moving Things Forward

Show up as the Knight (the Action taker) – continued to be guided by your team.

Four of Swords – After the big confrontation, things go a bit quiet. You take some time to re-group and calm down. Decisions must be made though. The Knight of Swords helps you to put emotions aside and do what needs to be dealt with. Legal advice is taken and you report your neighbour to the local planning office.

Five of Swords

Five in Tarot marks the first difficulty in the first stage of any journey. Here in the challenging Mental Realm, it refers to the aftermath of a battle of some kind. You can't fix this situation with your neighbour. It's very unpleasant and you're still furious and resentful. Again, your Major Arcana coaches are on the side lines. There has to be some degree of acceptance here; however things play out with the authorities, there have been losses. The anger you are feeling is justifiable but there's nowhere to put it. Things don't move quickly and there's a long difficult period while your neighbour shows no interest or remorse about the situation. He feels confident that he will win – and maybe he will, you just don't know. All you can do is deal with what is. As the Knight you are still determined to push through this log jam and fight in any way you can. The Temperance card and the Devil both have important comments to make here. It's important that you don't let your anger control you; the temptation to take revenge, to feel better and snatch back some power is powerful. Remember, Swords bring with them a double-edged capability; the Knight energy in the suit of Swords can be difficult to control. These two Majors counsel against allowing emotions (anger) to get too dominant. Swords hate emotion and, in his attempt to get back control, the Knight energy can be 'overzealous'.

Stage Three – Taking It Forward

Show up as the Queen of Swords (Self Control) – continue to be guided by your team.

Six of Swords

This wall situation has been absolutely horrible. The fact is, in reality, it feels like a no-win scenario. The acceptance suggested by the Hanged Man, Death and the balance that Temperance suggests have been tough to swallow but it's obvious that there is actually no choice. All we can do here is focus on our own situation. As we transition our energy from the Knight to the Queen of Swords, we find ourselves embodying the very essence of the suit. There is a cold, hard, grittiness to this, but the tough love Queen of Swords is pragmatic rather than hot headed. Anger has cooled by necessity into icy practicality. We know that we are going to have to move on from this sooner or later (Death). Our legal battle may be over, or it may be continuing, but either way, the damage has been done. We do have to get on with it. This current phase asks us to really bring our emotions in check so that perhaps an agreement might be reached (Temperance). Is there a possibility for some kind of mediation? Maybe, or maybe not, but now is the time to explore options. Is there a way that entrenched positions might be re-evaluated now some time has passed? (The Hanged Man).

Seven of Swords

Coming to terms with your neighbour's dishonest behaviour and his blatant stealing of your garden space has been a challenge. The wall is still in place, and it reminds you every day that life isn't fair. Perhaps you have envisaged revenge, imagining ways in which you can regain some power or at least take the shine off his apparent victory. The Devil tells you that this is a distraction, a temptation that could very possibly escalate things further. The Tower asks you who you really are. Perhaps you haven't seen this side of yourself before and it shocks you that you could even think of some of the scenarios that you are playing with in your head. As the Queen of Swords, you are not going to stoop to such lows, though. What you really want is to escape the situation altogether, to run away but you can't right now — or can you? Perhaps you should move house? It's a bitter pill to swallow, but the Queen of Swords begins by taking control of herself and her reactions. You can't avoid tough decisions and you can't just run away, but you can choose your own thoughts, make decisions about what this means for you and perhaps whether or not you even want to live there anymore.

Stage Four — Making It Real and Owning It

Show up as the King of Swords — taking executive control based on evidence to enable confident decision making.

Eight of Swords

The trouble is, you don't want to move really, and there are lots of factors in play. Maybe house prices have gone up, the kids' schools are nearby and they have local friends, but that wretched wall doesn't look great in your garden. But it's not comfortable living next to your neighbour who has caused all this trouble. Everything feels destabilised (the Tower says it happens, you can rebuild) and it feels like things have changed.

The happiness you used to feel living in the house has been

tainted (Death says everything changes, nothing stays the same). The decision to stay or to go is a tough one – the King of Swords steps back and tells you to make an executive decision. Rather than overthinking everything, really look at the facts. It's not easy, you don't really want to leave but you also don't want to stay here.

The King advises you to just decide one way or another, and you decide you will make it work, one way or another. If we are guided by the Hanged Man's advice, perhaps we can see that a move might be a new start. Also, perhaps things aren't quite resolved legally, maybe your neighbour will be forced to move the wall, but maybe not. Perhaps there will be a decision made that will decide things, but even if that's the case, your relationship with your neighbour is broken. Round and round you go, unable to think things through. The King advises you again to take control of your thoughts and manage the way you're thinking. Make what decision you can make and allow everything else to happen in its own time. Overthinking isn't solving anything right now. In fact, it's actually making things even worse.

Nine of Swords

As your mind goes into overdrive, you start worrying about everything. What if you can't sell the house? You'll be stuck there and will have to see your neighbour every day, forever! What if you move and the kids have to move school; what if they hate it and you've ruined their lives; what if nothing changes and this situation just continues indefinitely? What if you lose the court case and your neighbour actually wins? It feels unbearable. It wakes you up in the middle of night and plays every nightmare through in grim detail. The King's energy is absolutely necessary here to guide your thoughts back to evidence only. Fear is running the show; what we are afraid of is more pain. The Devil here is guidance on the fact that you have become hypnotised by a horror story that is playing out in your head. You think you 'need' to swim around in this sea of anxiety, but you don't. Your five guides are there as signposts. The Hanged Man asks you to stop running the stories in your head; Death asks you to let go of what has been and prepare for something new; Temperance says while it's not black and white, perhaps we can create something new that will be the right mix for everyone. The Tower once again says trust yourself; you are stronger than you know. Who are you really in all this? Is a family conference the way forward here, where all the facts are laid out clearly, so that difficult decisions can be made and proper strategies can be implemented?

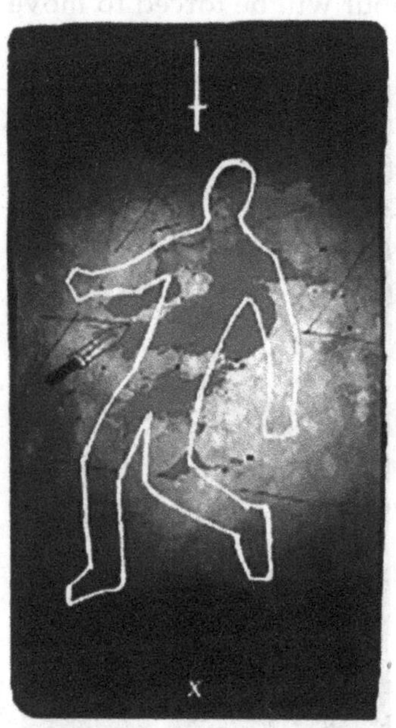

Ten of Swords

When we become a victim of our own thoughts, we become a victim of life. For sure, life sometimes sucks, that's fact, but when we allow ourselves to descend into a sea of fear and hurt, we can't make any clear decisions. A crime has been committed, perhaps by a third party. Perhaps you genuinely feel badly treated and you're still angry – but to commit a further crime against yourself by becoming lost in the fog of fear and pain is to grant that situation complete power over your life. Using the energy of the King of Swords we can avoid becoming a victim of life. Learning to master our minds and the way we think gives us back the power that situations beyond our control can rob us of. Remember your Ace imperative, that desire to solve and transcend the problem. Each of the five Majors in this Realm guide us through the process of doing just that. The King of Swords holds the key though, one clear thought at a time. One Sword is all you can use at a time; learn to use it well and you can always fight your way back.

Chapter 21

A Reading for Dhruv

Dhruv had been struggling for some time to find his way to a life experience that felt confident and enriching to him. He was still living with his parents, but was not finding that easy and wanted to make the move to a more independent life experience. His parents were not exactly supportive of his plans to move in with his girlfriend, so there had been some considerable conflict about this subject already. He was not feeling optimistic about life and pretty miserable about his situation. His question was:

'How should I move forward to a more independent life in the best possible way?'

His 'You Are Here' card was the Five of Swords.

This did rather sum up Dhruv's feelings about life right now. He felt like he was caught in the middle of a no-win situation and whatever he did it would not end well.

We can see on the card a scene that looks like the aftermath of a battle. Two figures stand back-to-back next to a grave. There is bitterness, sadness and it is not clear who has won and who has lost. The poppies (lest we forget) tell us that memories of this event will be long, and hurt will not be forgotten easily. All this does not make for a simple solution, but it tells Dhruv that he can't fix things by staying in the same energy. He must choose a way forward, make a decision one way or the other and leave this energy in the past, accepting that it's going to take quite some time for things to heal whatever he does.

His Royal significator is therefore the Knight of Swords.

The Knight of Swords is a card of action, and that action is not fuelled by emotion but by the desire to get something done. Emotions are not something our Knight of Swords fighter pilot is interested in. Going into battle and being prepared to fight for what you want is never easy. We must be careful with the Knight of Swords energy, though, it's a powerful surge of energy that can – if used thoughtlessly – do more harm than good. All Swords cards are double edged though, so we must make sure 'thoughtless' is not on the agenda. Being prepared to communicate clearly and fearlessly, though, is.

Guidance for His Primary Focus?
Death (Internal Process)

Death represents change and endings. Letting go of what must end is a really hard ask but that's the focus of Dhruv's reading, really. Dhruv's parents don't want to let him go, they don't want their relationship with him to change, he doesn't want to hurt them, but also doesn't want to stay the same. In order for him to start a new life with his girlfriend, his old life will have to die to make way for it. His parents will have to grieve; he will have to grieve because his relationship with them will change. Death sits within the Mental Realm, because how we use our mind to make sense of the situation will be the deciding factor. If Dhruv just lets all his conflicting emotions call the shots, he won't be able to make the decisions he has to. Death requires us to accept difficult emotions but not let them stop the process of change, which actually in the longer term is best for everyone concerned.

Expanded Reading

Court Card - Suggested Significator

Minor Arcana - Past Process (Losing Power)

YOU ARE HERE

Minor Arcana - Future Process - (Gaining Power)

Major Arcana - Stay On Track

Major Arcana - The Road Ahead

Primary Focus

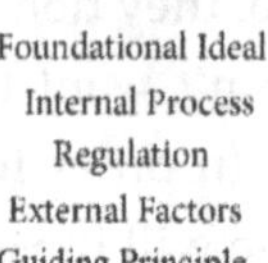

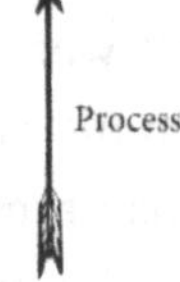

Foundational Ideal
Internal Process
Regulation
External Factors
Guiding Principle

Process

As we can see from the above spread, Dhruv has a difficult situation on his hands. As to how to move forward ... let's see what the rest of the reading advises.

Past, Present and Future

We can see a really clear picture of Dhruv's journey, from the row that brought him to the point he is now. The Three of Swords is always a hard card to manage, there is often a build-up of past tension or conflict that is being expressed in this falling out. There are often words which, once spoken, cause ripples of hurt along the timeline and we can see that reflected in the current situation of the Five of Swords. The Four of Swords describes the withdrawal that Dhruv has made to try and bring everything back to balance. For a while, he just tried to not engage with the problem at all, even now keeping his thoughts to himself, trying not to make the situation worse, but he can't keep quiet for ever.

Moving forward, we can see Dhruv in the transitionary phase of the Six of Swords, making plans to move away and dealing with the emotional situation as best he can. The Six of Swords is not a fast-moving card, though. He has the Knight of Swords as his significator so is advised to move quickly and decisively when the time is right. If he doesn't, he may lose momentum. The Seven of Swords tells him that he will probably be tempted to keep his plans to himself, moving stealthily until he can make a move that cannot be challenged, or that he will encounter strategies from his parents that are designed to block whatever action he is planning to take. It is often a card associated with escape; of not confronting what you need to face properly. The Seven of Swords is a card of tactics; no-one is being honest at this point.

Death, as Dhruv's primary focus is the internal system that will help him in his situation. It is supported by the other Majors in the Mental Realm.

Guidance to Stay on Track

The Hanged Man tells Dhruv that patience may be necessary here. It also asks Dhruv what he is prepared to give up in the process. He will have to sacrifice something if things are going to change. The Hanged Man does offer a change of perspective with time. Perhaps his parents will see things differently with a different approach, or as they get used to this new situation? Perhaps Dhruv will need to give up trying to control the whole scenario, just decide what he is going to and do it. The Knight of Swords certainly seems to support that approach.

Temperance suggests trying to find a solution that calms things down. Perhaps Dhruv needs to talk things through again with his parents. He does not want to alienate them from his life, but would still like to be able to have a private life of his own.

The Knight of Swords is a card of action, of clear communication, but it does need to be handled with care. If Dhruv can be seen to have a plan that doesn't abandon his parents, just allows him the independence he wants, perhaps the right balance can be found. Perhaps he will tell them he will not move too far away; perhaps he will promise regular visits. Whatever is right for him that helps everyone feel heard and understood.

Guidance for the Road Ahead

The Devil is an interesting card; it is at its core a selfish instinct, and also speaks of attachments which are not healthy. Co-dependant relationships are very much within the remit of the Devil's energy. If we return to the Devil as the external influence on the situation, we can see how that might be relevant. It will be important for Dhruv to figure out where the real love is in this scenario and what is simply controlling or selfish. Those limiting versions of love are often just fear, working behind the scenes in disguise. Making decisions from a position of love, without fear calling the shots for all concerned, will help Dhruv know what's real and what's not. The Devil card encourages you to look at your shadow side, what might you be tempted to do to avoid discomfort – those actions are never made from a position of honesty and kindness. There is a warning here not to get sucked into doing things for the wrong reasons, it will ultimately only make things worse not better.

The Tower as the guiding principle for the process is the truth that we are forced to see about ourselves and our situation. When we ask the question about love, we are looking at what the truth really is behind the drama. Dhruv is having to redefine himself in the light of his parents' reaction: who is he in all of this? How will he move forward if his parents continue to react as they have been? Sometimes, of course, life surprises you in a good way. Perhaps by taking down the existing structure of their collective relationship, a new relationship can be built over time; a more loving tolerant, respectful relationship that can endure and take care of everyone's needs. Sometimes we have to let things fall, in order for them to be rebuilt.

Finally, the Rod gives us the process by which the Death card itself is constructed.

The Moon in the Experience Realm gives us the environment that makes Death so difficult. Having to walk through the 'dark', not knowing where the light is, challenges the best of us. As a component of Death, the Moon reminds Dhruv that he must be able to trust himself and his connection to the energetic world to guide him through this dark experience. This will keep him going even though he is afraid, and will allow the process of letting go to take him to the next stage.

Strength in the Energetic Realm advises him to not try and control or react against the process, but instead put his attention inside to bring himself back in to balance. The process is not an easy one and he must take care of himself in the process.

The Empress in the Emotional Realm reminds us that we (male or female) are the creative hub from which all new life springs. We can always find ways to creatively renew ourselves, comfort ourselves and find pleasure in life even in small ways, even if life is challenging in the extreme. Again, this brings Dhruv back to the idea of love. If he knows that he has Strength enough not to break in those times, even if he feels bent in two, he can allow himself to have compassion — for not only himself but all concerned. This will support him and the process of uncomfortable change and letting go in the best way possible.

Chapter 22

The Experience Realm

Nothing ever becomes real until it is experienced.
John Keats

Ruled by the Suit of Pentacles and the Element of Earth

Pentacles are our experience of life. Pentacles are represented by the element of earth, referring quite literally to the place where we make it real; where we bring it 'down to earth'. We build on the earth and the earth is the place from which all things grow. When we take a feeling then apply our will and our mind to it, we create an experience in real life. Every experience we create builds into further experiences, and this becomes our overall life experience. We then share experiences, trading them to improve our overall experience. Experience is the real currency with which we create our lives, and it's the quality of the experiences we have that creates our life abundance.

In the Beginning There Was an Ace

At the start of every Tarot journey is the Ace, a gift, an opportunity for something new to happen. Here in the suit of Pentacles the Ace gives the seed that could grow into a new experience of abundance in our life, an opportunity to build something of value, adding to our experience of wealth. This is the vision of the potential we see as the Ten of Pentacles. In this little picture, we imagine our quality of life being upgraded in a meaningful way, maybe feeling a little more secure, a little more excited because of the extra things we will be able to do or add to our lives.

This picture may not be the whole long-term deal but it's another step on the journey to when life is just 'sorted'. That vision will be informed by our experiences so far and what we feel is possible. This isn't just the romantic flash of the Ten of Cups. The Ace of Pentacles is the combination of all three other suits so while, yes, we can see enhanced happiness in this picture, we also get a little excited, imaginative Wands flash of things you're going to 'do'; but also present is the more gritty Swords element. This new opportunity may lead us outside our comfort zone — and there may be some fear in the mix and some problems to solve.

The Ace of Pentacles is — by nature of it being ruled Pentacles — the element of earth, the most literal 'seed' Ace of all the aces. It is inherently slow in the realisation of its potential and will need us to bring all the parts of ourselves to the table to make it successful. It's the classic acorn from which great oaks grow, and that oak we are growing is the tree of our life.

The Role of the Royals — in the Minor Arcana Suit of Pentacles

Let's look at the Royals in the suit of Pentacles and how they refer to us personally, showing us how we can use and embody the energy of the Pentacles suit effectively, learning and gaining experience until we are able to operate as the King.

Once again, we can see how the Royals respond to the changing requirements of the progressional Minors. We are being asked to show up or approach things in different ways for different situations. The Royals tell us exactly how to manage the journey through each Realm to make sure we get the best result possible.

The Page (the Student) — Two and Three of Pentacles

The inspiration of the Ace in the suit of Pentacles is to build an abundant secure life experience that is sustainable, as described in the Ten of Pentacles. The Page of Pentacles is the most academic of the Tarot Pages; he is curious about the processes involved in building that Ten of Pentacles experience.

Twos in Tarot refer to a situation that is still needing choices to be made and further development. The Two of Pentacles describes a fluid situation where we find ourselves moving our attention between two different experiences, so our situation is in some way unformed and unstable. We must adapt to this and be flexible to its requirements.

Rather than judge this as good or bad, the Page just enjoys whatever the experience offers. He still remains curious, learning about what is and is not possible with regard to its longer potential and how much ultimately to invest in it. In a way, the Two of Pentacles is an important lesson on the skill of flexibility within itself. How flexible and adaptable to change we are, will be important as we move through life.

Conversely, perhaps we have learned to be too flexible? What is the right balance? What are the choices we should make in our quest to create a life experience that we will enjoy and can sustain? It's all an experiment here, but our conclusions will count as the stakes get higher throughout life.

In the Three of Pentacles, the Page adds his newly learned experience to enrich and expand what is often a pre-existing situation. The Three of Pentacles is the classic 'job' card – we are joining a team. Again, the Page uses the situation to add value and gain experience. He only has limited power here and it's not a life choice, so it's important that he learns what he needs to and moves on once the situation has reached its maximum potential for growth.

The inspiration of the Ace to make a life experience that is rich and sustainable is complex in the suit of Pentacles, and the process of building that life means adding and building valuable experience over a period of time. The Page's job is to learn about which experiences are enriching and worth investing in and which are depleting and need to be moved on from. This he learns in the Two and Three of Pentacles. We need to try things to see if they work, we can only learn if we 'do' but we must actually learn as a result, or our overall experience will quickly become poorer for it.

The Knight (the Action) – Four and Five of Pentacles

The Knights tell us about the energy required to move things forward. There is often little reference to courage when we talk about the suit of Pentacles, and the Knight especially is often seen as the least exciting of all the Tarot Knights. When we look at Pentacles through the lens of 'experience' though, we can see that the temptation to hang on to what we've got in

the Four of Pentacles can be very powerful indeed. It takes courage to keep going, to keep building. To trade what we feel we have for the unrealised potential of something 'more' is a hard ask. The Four of Pentacles is a very definite confidence 'wobble'. Of course, it's important to stabilise, but having done so, the pull to stop and cut one's losses is more powerful here than in any other suit. The Knight of Pentacles keeps going; it's not a fast energy but it's determined and relentless. Pentacles give us the combination of all the suits together, so we must consider and balance the equation of our emotions, our drive and passion for more/ different and our logical head to make the decisions we need to, to keep going.

It's here the dreaded Five of Pentacles often undercuts our progress and kills our ability to take risks in life. 'Not enough' is the watchword of this card and it comes as a result of a lack of experience of 'better'. We plan our lives based on what our experience has been so far. We expect to experience more of the same and so often plan accordingly. This is why the Page of Pentacles is so foundational. In the Five of Pentacles energy, our 'Ace' vision of the Ten is poor, our expectations are low. Our experiences to date have taught us that we are not worthy or welcome in the world of more or better. It takes real courage to move through that mire. Courage, time spent in consistent effort and dogged determination. In this light, the Knight of Pentacles, in fact, appears to be the bravest of all the Tarot knights. He tells you to keep going, not to give up. It's not easy, but it's worth it.

The Queen (the Process) – Six and Seven of Pentacles

The Six of Pentacles is, as are all sixes in Tarot, a tipping point between stages. The 'lack' that is expressed in the Five of Pentacles is hard to overcome and takes time, as we can see in the energy of the Six and the Seven. As the Queen, we are asked to embody the energy of the suit, to become it. The suit of Pentacles is the experience created by our personal expression of each of the other suits. So, here, as the Queen of Pentacles, we are being asked to step into the very energy we want to create. When we change ourselves, we change our world experience. We can see the energy of all the Queens in play with the Queen of Pentacles energy, helping us to settle any internal problems we have around abundance by using each one to its best effect.

She manages to find the perfect compromise of practicality and emotion, aspiration and inspiration, with a decent helping of gritty resolve to get the job done. All the elements working together in harmony. This enables the tipping point of the Six to do its job. In the Six of Pentacles, we are asked to look at our own self-worth and how it informs the balance of power we experience in our lives. We may need some help at this stage, but it's important we do not become overly dependent on that help.

If we are in relationships that are not equal, that keep us wanting or needing more, we must reassess that situation. We come out of the Five of Pentacles in a state of need, but we must reduce that 'need' and we do that by changing our vision of who we are and what we are capable of. There is an inherent call for compromise in the energy of the Queen of Pentacles. The definition of compromise being 'to settle a dispute by mutual concession'. As the Queen, therefore, we are asked to find compromises within ourselves by dealing with our emotions and short-term needs, getting practical by building confidence and courage, and using our objectivity to strategise in order to create a new vision of who we are and what we're worth.

Moving into the Seven of Pentacles, we spend time assessing our progress. It might be that it feels like the investments we have made improving our experience of life feel slow to realise. Sevens in Tarot are usually a bit frustrating, leaving us with no concrete plan, just a continuing exploration as to what might constitute a realistic way forward. We can't go back so we must re-commit ourselves to this new energy. The Queen's gentle but pragmatic approach will help sustain us through that process.

The Queen of Pentacles' energy enables us to straddle that line between aspiration for the future and the practicalities of our current situation. Because she embodies the perfect combination of all the energy, she creates the perfect environment for success within herself while taking care of the emotional needs of those depending on her. The aspiration of the Ten of Pentacles is a long-term plan which involves family and connection. We are in the process of building ourselves into the version of ourselves that will support everyone. So this isn't just a selfish endeavour. Keeping

the vision clear now, remembering the reason we are on this journey and making what compromises we must when we must, will bear fruit and we will see the results play out over time.

The King (the Management) – Eight and Nine of Pentacles

It's here we must start to raise our game, we must expand and build further. We have done the groundwork within ourselves, and now we must put all we've learned to work and step up as the King.

The Eight and Nine of Pentacles is really the home straight on the Pentacles journey. The work done as the Queen, needs to be properly managed and applied in the real world if this Ten of Pentacles aspiration is indeed to become a reality. This is not a journey that happens overnight, as we know; Pentacles are slow because we are trying to build something that lasts and endures. We understand the Eight of Pentacles as a process of perseverance, continued learning and up-skilling. We are told that to become a 'master' in any skill takes 10,000 hours of dedication and practice. This is the process described in the Eight of Pentacles. Money management is of course a major focus in the Pentacles suit, making money and being able to both keep it and make more of it while enjoying our increased abundance are huge drivers in our Ten of Pentacles goal, but while that's important, it's more than that. It's a mistake to see Pentacles as purely financial. Creating the experience of a 'rich life' is far broader than that. It's about having the power to make a life that brings you happiness, fulfilment and some excitement – a life of your own choosing.

We can see the King of Pentacles as a very down to earth version of the Magician. Being able to create a life that feels rich and satisfying takes perseverance and skill. The King makes his life experience better and better by honing every part of life, and in creating the environment of the abundant life experience we see in the Nine, we can see that this also informs those around him. He has the opportunity to enrich the lives of many others, whether they be family, friends, employees, contractors, retailers etc. In the Nine of Pentacles he can create and enrich his environment with the choices he makes and the lifestyle he chooses. Personal power brings personal responsibility though, so with all the Tarot Kings in play, hopefully he can balance all the elements in each of the suits to create a richer experience for all.

The Ten of Pentacles refers to family, clan and legacy. Remember that the Ten of Cups ideal is also contained at the root of why we are doing this; it's in the Pentacles DNA. This is no empty, dry financial aspiration. This is the big deal that is at the root of most human aspiration. A happy, financially secure life experience that can be handed on to those we love, laying the ground for future generations to benefit feeling secure in the knowledge that 'The World' we have created is a success for all concerned.

Chapter 23

The Role of Experience Realm Majors

The Matrix of an Abundant Life Experience

The Majors in each Realm give us the method by which we navigate to our goal of a successful outcome. They are the matrix for achieving the confidence and staying power we need to make things happen. They give us the words of advice we need to be wise and to get the best outcome when approaching new ideas, projects or aspirations. If we follow their guidance, we won't go far wrong. Each Major gives us a different perspective on the way to achieve our ideal.

1. The Foundational Ideal – the rock on which we stand and from which we navigate towards our goal.
2. The Internal Process – What we need to actually do within and for ourselves to achieve that goal.
3. Regulation – The way we set the rules we need, both for ourselves and around external influences to successfully achieve our outcome.
4. The External Regulation – What will influence and exert control over us externally on the route to our goal.
5. Guiding Principle – This is the north star that helps us steer our path to a successful outcome.

The Foundational Ideal — the Star

As the foundational ideal in our Ace vision of that aspirational Ten of Pentacles experience, the Star is the beacon of hope that enables us to visualise a future, to build and to keep going. It tells us that the foundation we must hold as the ideal base to build from is the trust we have in ourselves and our intuitive sense. This is going to be fundamental if we want to create a life experience that is happy and abundant. If we have no experience of trust or faith that we can always rebuild, always start again and find a way to ultimately solve whatever problems we must to reach a life experience that is happy and fulfilling, we simply find ourselves stuck and unable to move forward. This makes the foundational experience of trust the bedrock on which all things stand. The Star is the ideal of our Pentacles journey — the dream on which all things are built and the faith that you have in yourself that you can make them real.

- I trust myself and my ability to always rebuild and work through any challenge life throws at me.
- I have faith in my own process and the energy that works around me.
- My life experience is a work in progress.
- In the face of no evidence, I know that there is more to come for me.

The Internal Process — the Moon

Being able to confront both your light and your shadow is vital if we are going to create the experience of our choosing. The

Moon in Tarot refers to the parts of ourselves that we often keep hidden, our fears about life, what is and isn't possible, and fears about ourselves, usually because we believe certain aspects of us are not useful or acceptable, making us in some way unlovable to others and also again, to ourselves. This is the part of us that Carl Jung called our 'shadow self'. Going inside and finding out exactly what is in that basement part of ourselves is an adventure that most of us decide not to embark on. Fear sets up horror movies ahead of us on the path, and these illusions are designed to stop us in our tracks and keep us from moving forward or changing our life experience in any meaningful way. Using the foundational ideal of trust at the root of everything, we can experience our fear and know we'll be OK, we'll work it out somehow. This enables us to move from the safe space of the Three of Pentacles through the increasingly challenging process of the Four and the Five of Pentacles. We are being asked to confront the fear of our own lack full on. Our fears only have power over us because we choose to keep them hidden, both from public view and from our own internal gaze. Coming face to face with that which we fear is not easy, but it's vital because if we don't, our fear always has one hand on the steering wheel of the car. In this way it influences the route and ultimately therefore chooses the destination.

The Moon's advice is around how we respond internally to create our experience.

- My fear is not my truth.
- I can move forward through and in spite of my fear.
- I choose to give my fear compassion but no power.
- Fear doesn't care about my happiness.

Regulation – the Sun

Our experience of joy is not something most of us are encouraged to explore. We often see it as an optional extra in life, to be experienced

in fleeting moments while we move through the stress of real life. Real joy comes from an experience of life that is not informed by fear. When we are not afraid, we find we can see beyond the mundane, the worry, the voice inside that chats in our head constantly, about what's wrong, what went wrong in the past and what might go wrong in the future. When we trust ourselves and are not living with fear running the show, we are free to be in the moment, to focus on what is really important, which is our own energy. If we live by the theory that our external experience is actually a reflection of our internal world, we can see how important it is to create a joyful internal experience for ourselves, because that will, in turn, manifest as our experience of life.

Using the benchmark of joy as our regulation, we can start to make decisions about what elements are in our life because we are afraid and start to question what we actually want to do, what we want to create as a life experience that would bring more joy into our overall experience. If we define joy as being the absence of fear, we can start to imagine how a life without the shadow of fear might feel. This is the light that guides us through the Five of Pentacles and beyond into the next stage of the Six, Seven and Eight of Pentacles. All kinds of new questions might arise; if I was not afraid, what would I do? If we go back to the Ten of Pentacles as the successful, happy, abundant life experience that Tarot leads us towards, we can see how joyful that is as a destination. Happiness and contentment comes from a feeling of being lovingly connected to friends and family, within an overall life experience that is rich, sustainable and pleasurable. Joy is the theme that runs like a river through these experiences. When we can see life clearly through that lens, when we regulate our lives from that perspective, we can see life for what it really is: a miracle of existence, an adventure of ups and downs through the incredible landscapes of our life. We automatically gravitate toward experiences that add real value to our lives, guided by the joy we are always looking to create.

The Sun's advice is around our ability to experience joy.

- Joy is my default state and the place from which I make all my decisions.
- Joy is the place I always return to.
- I understand that I cannot experience real joy if the shadow of fear is present.
- I choose to see life as joyful and to create more joy both for myself and those around me.
- Today, I am overflowing with energy and full of joy.

External Regulation – Wisdom

We become wise through our experiences, through 'doing'; we then receive feedback from the external results of those things we've done. Practical experience is the key to success in life. The lessons of the past then regulate our decisions as we move forward. Knowing that we are where we are because of the decisions we've taken in the past can be seen as either positive or negative. The fact is though, if we see everything as being perfectly aligned to guide us to a better life experience, we can take advantage of all that experience we've had to date and put it to work in the next chapter of our life experience. We persevere at life, and carry on making it better and better, until we get to an experience that is enriching and enjoyable, and we can see how this directly informs process through the Eight and Nine of Pentacles.

Being able to leave the past behind and begin again with the benefit of experience is a skill that is learnt over time. To be able to build experience and wisdom from our own life experiences then apply those lessons to the path ahead gives us tremendous power. We do this with our experience of the previous three cards. By trusting ourselves, by not allowing fear to drive the bus and by knowing what a joyful life feels like. This way we can look back at where we've come from, all we've done, our successes, our failures, our happiness, our disappointments, our wins and losses, and not be defined by any of them. The past has no place in the present, but the experience that we gain from it can be used to make the rules moving forward. If we're not going to repeat the same mistakes again and again, we must be able to make new rules and behave in new ways. So, whether we're experiencing good times or bad, we know how to keep our compass pointing in the right direction, towards that lovely aspirational Ten.

Wisdom gives us advice on moving on from the past with wisdom.

- Today, I leave behind my old habits and adopt new helpful ones.
- I am confident in my judgement and can handle situation as they arise and make good decisions.
- The past has no place in the present.
- I have evolved into the version of myself that I always wanted to be.
- I forgive those who have caused me pain in my past and let them go peacefully.
- I know life allows for endless re-inventions of my experience, and if I lean into change and expansion, life will respond in kind.

Guiding Principle – the World

'The World' card, as the final card in the Major Arcana, is often seen as the destination card. In readings, it refers to a successful conclusion, a 'congratulations, you've done it' moment. It refers to mastery and as seeing something as 'as good as it gets'.

All of this holds sway as well when we see 'the World' card as the guiding principle in our journey to the Ten Of Pentacles. In fact, they are really one and the same. 'The World' is where it all comes together, everything working as it should. As the Master Magician at this point, we can see we have done our job well, embodying the energy of the four Kings, each helping to create the real world experience that we actually want. The guiding principle of life mastery in action.

This also tells us to aim high in all matters. If we see Pentacles as the perfect mix of the other three suits, 'the World' becomes a signpost for that perfect combination of elements that would specifically make your life a happy and successful one.

It also advises that you work from the principle that you don't accept less than you think is possible. The question is though, what *do* you think is possible? This will set the parameters of what can be created. If our external world is a reflection of our internal world, the World card refers to the best we have inside us, which in turn will create our personal life experience.

So, 'the World' is *not* the final destination, it's a construct which can be constantly re-evaluated. We are often taught that the Fool, having arrived at 'the World', is born again. This is often presented as the moment of spiritual ascension. But if we look at it in terms of real life, we can see it as a 'level up' moment, where we make our world a bit better.

If we focus on that wisdom that we have gained from our past experiences that created more joy and more abundance in our lives, choosing to turn away from those that have produced the opposite, we can start again at the next stage and make a new happier, richer world experience for ourselves. The question is, how good at the game of life can we get?

In truth, 'the World' as our guiding principle in creating our joyful, rich, abundant life refers to both our current world and the one we want to create. We must decide what is within us, what we have learned, what we aspire to and 'the World' we create as a result will be, in effect, 'as good as it gets'.

Tarot tells us everything is always moving and changing, *we* are always moving and changing, so if we use the experience of 'the World' as our inspiration and our instruction manual, we can always continue to raise our game. We learn to play smarter, getting wiser, happier and more abundant, continuing to build that Ten of Pentacles experience for ourselves and those we love with everything we've got.

The World gives us advice on building a successful abundant sustainable life experience.

- I am the architect of my life and everything in it.
- I love and accept myself for who I am.
- I believe I can, so I do.
- I celebrate and am grateful for all the abundance in my life.

- I believe in myself.
- I am a success.
- Every day I become more confident, powerful, and successful.

Putting It All Together in the Experience Realm

Let's look at the journey through the Minor Arcana suit of Pentacles from the perspective of a student beginning his journey. The story we're going to tell here is the creation of a life path. The Minor Arcana will lead the way, giving up the basic process and the stages we will need to go through. The Royals will advise us as to the energy we can best show up in to make the best of each stage most effectively, and the Majors act as the coaches, standing on the sidelines shouting helpful advice to help us build our expertise and experience in order that we can achieve our goal.

Chapter 24

Once Upon a Time, There Was a Student

Your **Ace of Pentacles,** like all aces, carries within it a dream, a vision of the potential of something wonderful. This Ace is a special seed though. If we stay with the analogy of the acorn that carries within it the DNA of a 300-year-old oak tree, it is complex. It needs to be planted in the right place away from mowers, or nibbling creatures, or landscape gardeners with entirely another vision in mind. It needs the right soil to grow in and the right amount of warmth, light and water and it needs time because this is a slow-growing seed that can take a lifetime to bear its own fruit. The fruit that the Ace of Pentacles promises is a life experience that is happy, fulfilling, financially secure and connected. A life we are happy to be in and to have lived. A life in which we feel a sense of achievement, and in which we have made a difference. This is the holy grail, the definition of a life well lived. Every seed is different, each carries a different version of this potential life, represented by the aspiration of the Ten of Pentacles.

Our story here is about Josh, a young chap who is just off to university. We might see him as the Fool at the start of a new journey, full of potential, not really knowing what to expect and not thinking much farther ahead than getting there and getting this new life experience underway. Once he begins his journey for real though, he stands in the role of the Magician, young and inexperienced in the power that he has to create in life. His most important lessons are not so much the academic knowledge that the degree promises, but self-knowledge, his approach to life, how he learns and makes decisions. He must develop a vision of himself and use his abilities to make every experience work for him in the most positive way. This is not an easy undertaking, but it's one we must all make.

Stage One — Learning and Exploring

Two of Pentacles — This is the first stage of development.

The Page of Pentacles is the quintessential student so, here, as Josh goes about the business of learning about his potential life path, it's important he stays open and curious about the experience he is both having and wants to build moving forward. During this process he might find himself to be not quite as clear about things as he would have hoped. Juggling a part-time job with studying can make it hard to concentrate. Perhaps he decided to swap subjects midway through. There are also a myriad of distractions in terms of friendships, love affairs, money worries and deadlines that can make life feel like a plate-spinning contest. It is in this place, though, he starts to learn about the life experience he might ultimately want — or not want? A part-time entry level job might give some experience that can be built on, but what does he want to build? Probably not that. This balancing act will/must ultimately end, and decisions will have to be made. This student entry-level lifestyle can only continue for so long before things start to feel stale.

Three of Pentacles – Expansion and implementation.

After his life as a student ends, our young Josh must move to the next stage. While he may not be an actual student anymore, he is still very definitely learning. Here, as we reach the Three of Pentacles, our youngster is learning about life in a real full-time job with a medium-sized building contractor responsible for local municipal works. The little bit of experience he gained while working through college, plus his completed construction engineering qualification, meant he could move to the next level and start earning some money. This job may not be his heart's desire though, he's still at the beginning of things, but he is at least gaining more experience. He learns about working as part of a team. He has a role to play and he must fulfil that role or lose the job. He will learn a lot about himself during this time, how he sees himself, his future and what he thinks is possible for him.

If we consult our guides, the Majors, through these two cards, their advice may well be to check in with how he is feeling about things. As he moves through university and his first job, does he have a feeling of hope and optimism about the future; does he trust himself to work out a route? Is he afraid he might not be in the right place? Perhaps afraid he is not good enough, or won't be chosen, or fit in in some way? Does he enjoy what he does, does he feel empowered and confident, does life feel positive and possible? Where is this path leading? How does success on this path look — inviting and exciting or grey, gritty and boring?

Stage Two — Moving Things Forward

Four of Pentacles — Stabilisation and conservation.

The Four of Pentacles imbues life with a feeling of caution. As Josh continues on this journey, he has found a satisfactory place to be. He has a little money, not a huge paycheque, but just about enough for his needs. He is OK at his job, which is OK enough to warrant not wanting to lose it. The question is, what should he do next, if anything? Using the energy of the Knight of Pentacles to keep going through this period will pay off. Although the Knight of Pentacles is probably the slowest (it's Pentacles after all) of all the Knights, he stays the course, moving slowly but surely through a process of planning and implementing.

In order to decide what to do next, our Josh must constantly refer back to his original Ace vision. Remember, the Pentacles refer to the experience created by the combination of all the suits. So he must tune into and take seriously how he feels, what he wants and what his passions are, and he must be able to think objectively and clearly to make decisions about what his next steps are. He has become more interested in housing and sustainability and would really like to be more involved in the design process. Of course, that's easier said than done and there is pressure on him from those around him, to do well, to be ambitious — or maybe that pressure is to be sensible and to recognise life's limitations and to hang on to what he's got.

Each of our Majors have points to make in this situation. The Star asks him:

What do you really want in life? Trust your own vision, what experience is important to you? How much faith do you have that life can work with you and not against you? The Moon asks him to explore any fears that come up as he answers that question. The Sun asks, what would feel good to you? Is there a version of life that you can see that fills you with enough enthusiasm to take some brave steps? Wisdom asks him to draw on his experience so far and to ask himself what this has taught him; that he can always start again or change his mind if he wants to. The World asks him to look at what he has created so far; is he happy with his progress? What does the idea of success feel like and what might it look like in the future? The Knight reminds him that whatever he thinks is possible will define what he does, and that will create the world he lives in down the years of his life. It tells him to keep going and just know that he's not there yet.

Five of Pentacles – Feelings of lack and 'not enough'.

Five in Tarot marks the first difficulty in the first stage of any journey. Here in the Experience Realm, our Josh is experiencing some problems with his confidence. It's been a few years now since he started his journey. To be honest, life is not shaping up in the way he hoped it might. Things didn't just work out; he wasn't chosen for the promotion he hoped would come his way and he's starting to feel like money is a problem. His confidence has taken a real knock and he is starting to question his own abilities. He's not really being terribly proactive, though, in his own life in general and that isn't helping. He doesn't feel 'enough' on any level. Not enough confidence and self-belief, not enough experience to feel he knows what to do next.

The Knight's energy here helps him keep going, even though progress is slow; that's what this particular Knight is good at – the hard yards! Josh simply must first decide he wants to change things. While of course he can't just wave a magic wand and simply make everything different overnight, he could still, with a bit of courage and self-reflection, make some better decisions about how he would like life to look moving forward. The Star advises him to know there is more to life than this, trust that if he starts making moves consistently, life will respond accordingly and show him the way forward. The Moon tells him that what is in his way is just his own fear. He is not seeing himself or life clearly. His low mood is a result of him not wanting to confront his own fears and insecurities for fear they might be real. The

Moon assures him they are not real, unless he decides to defend them himself, then of course he gets to keep them.

The Sun tells him for goodness' sake, 'lighten up'. Life is not supposed to be so grey. Even if things are not quite right at the moment, there is still fun to be had, there is still joy. Make it your job to decide to be happy and start walking toward that future, whatever that may be! Wisdom advises him to mentally go back to the beginning and retrace the steps he made, learn from what didn't work and form a new plan; other than that, leave the past behind, it doesn't need to define the future. The World says, 'You are complete with everything you need, life mastery is a big job, listen to the Knight and keep going. If you decide to work with us, you'll get there — wherever you decide "there" might be'.

Stage Three — Taking It Forward

Six of Pentacles — The tipping point between stages.

Josh is now a bit more grown up and has decided this life path he is currently on is simply not working. He has decided he could not get out of his situation on his own though. Finding a balance in life is not easy, and it's hard deciding how much power he really has to make things the way he wants them to be. He is finding out the hard way, as we all do. By using the energy of the Queen of Pentacles, he can observe the balance within himself. Balancing his emotions with his personal courage and willpower while getting his mental processes working in his favour is also not easy, but it's a necessary skill that, once he masters it properly, will serve him throughout life.

Josh is finally getting the message. He decides to meet with a friend of his who is successfully running his own business. Perhaps he can help? It takes some courage to talk to him – Josh is worried about looking too needy. But he shows up, nonetheless. The advice his friend gives changes everything. While his friend is not going to 'save' him, he does give him some sage words of advice about his life moving forward. He also suggests a change in attitude about life and a potential change of direction. This change will involve him making quite a serious investment of time and money in himself, as he repositions for this different potential future. But it offers a more inviting vision than the rather uninspiring path he is currently on.

The Star would advise that he trusts himself; he can always move forward and rebuild. The Moon suggests staying consciously aware of any fear that is making itself felt and dealing with it early. The Sun states that it's important to make sure his motivation feels positive and affirming and is not a response to fear, or it may not work in the way he wants. Wisdom reminds him not to repeat the past, it's time for a new approach now and the World advises him to have a clear picture of his destination and to know what it will look like when he successfully moves into this next place in his life.

Seven of Pentacles – Assessment of progress.

Still embodying that Queen of Pentacles energy, and armed with the information from his friend, Josh is considering the process of change. This, as with the rest of the journey, is not a quick undertaking. First, he has to decide *if* he is going to take action. But if not now, when? Looking at his Ten of Pentacles vision, he must decide who he is in that picture. He must be able to see the potential within himself to make any change happen. He instinctively understands that what he does now will decide what his future will be in the years to come.

Stage Four – Making It Real and Owning It

Eight of Pentacles – Upskilling and perseverance.

The next few years are pivotal. Josh makes the courageous decision to commit to a bold, audacious vision of his life. He decides to study to become an architectural engineer. He commits fully to this path and learns all he can about creating this experience in real life, studying and persevering. As he learns, he is stepping into the energy of the King of Pentacles. His passion is undeniable, and he completes his new qualification with honours. He is offered a role with a start-up firm of housing developers who are passionate about sustainable cutting-edge building. As he joins this new team, he begins to demonstrate a growing level of authority in the process. That gives those around him confidence, both in him personally and in his ability to handle whatever life throws at him. He really enjoys his new found confidence as his determination to solve problems and seek out innovative solutions becomes authority.

Those around him start to ask his opinion, and he begins to

contribute at a higher level, giving him significant financial reward in return. His confidence is built on his growing experience on his own abilities and his genuine passion for the business. He is known for his energy and positivity, his ability to plan, to manage, and his enthusiasm and vision to grow the company in new and exciting ways. The five Majors are a pivotal part of his handling of this process of gaining mastery. He trusts himself to be able to stay the course; he has faith in his own vision and is confident that he is moving in the right direction because he genuinely loves what he is doing. He knows now that he can figure things out when he must. He meets moments of fear and uncertainty with understanding and focus, approaching each new challenge or obstacle with patience and curiosity. He genuinely loves meeting these challenges and the people with whom he is interacting. He uses his growing level of experience to constantly adapt, becoming recognised overtime as an expert in his field.

Nine of Pentacles – Lifestyle and independence.

As Josh has grown in experience and expertise, as a result of all of the amassed experience, he is feeling pretty good about the life he has created. He has also attracted a higher level of financial reward, something he very much enjoys. The Nine of Pentacles refers to making a rich abundant life experience for yourself and this is exactly what has happened here. Josh now has a home he loves in an area that he finds enriching and enjoyable.

He has a level of financial security that means he feels secure and confident in his future. He enjoys regular holidays and a very decent level of comfort. All in all, a very nice lifestyle. It would be easy to badge this experience as being indulgent and, in many ways it is, but it was not easily obtained.

What this refers to is the process by which our experience quite literally becomes our currency. Experience is the means by which we become rich; whatever 'rich' means for you. A rich lifestyle may of course refer to luxury, financial independence and freedom, but it might also refer to living the life that you personally find enriching. The independence that this card implies represents our autonomy, our personal life experience and lifestyle. That encompasses not only enough financial security to make sure we feel happy and secure, but enough job satisfaction for us to feel engaged, stimulated and satisfied with our path.

The management energy of the King is important here, because maintaining this is a bigger job with many more decisions to make. We often see the King of Pentacles as being the consummate businessman and money maker. But while there is, of course, a powerful element of financial planning in any stable, enriching lifestyle, he's far more important than a mere businessman or money manager. The King of Pentacles can also be seen as the real-life embodiment of the Magician himself. The Magician's job is to master himself and his creative life energy in order to create the life that he himself chooses.

We often focus very heavily on money when we are reading the suit of Pentacles but money is just another form of energy and it represents for many of us the energy of abundance. The Magician's job is to be able to become a master creator with all the energies at play. So if we see the Magician as the physical embodiment of the Fool, the King of Pentacles becomes the real-life version of the Magician. He manages and controls all the suits, not just within himself but in his external world as well.

He understands and manages his emotional environment, making sure it is in accordance with the experience he feels good in; he understands the creative process within himself and manages his life energetically, with conscious intent and determination. He inspires and leads productively. He does all this by using his mind to steer effectively, never allowing any one thing to dominate, but creating a perfect mix of all the ingredients.

This is the point we are at as we reach level Nine in the suit of Pentacles. We can literally feel the end point of the Ten in sight. We get to experience much of that feeling of everything coming together and it might be easy to assume this is as good as it gets — because it is, indeed, pretty good. The difference between the Nine of Pentacles (and the Nine of Cups) and the Ten is the experience of sharing. Nines are our personal experience of the energy, but Ten takes us to a more connected experience, which makes it so much more satisfying.

Ten of Pentacles – All coming together.

Josh has done a great job and has built a life that is rich and satisfying. He has family now around him with longstanding meaningful friendships that have been built along the way. All of this evokes an understanding that he has built not only a stable, secure, comfortable life for himself, but also for those he loves and cares about. He has a sense of legacy. The work that he has done contributes to the lives of those he loves, and those whose lives are connected to his world in a meaningful way and that will outlast his own lifespan. He will be passing on not only his money, business and property, but also his ideology, his own experience of how to create an abundant life. This shared experience creates more abundance as the energy grows with a life of its own. This connectedness between people; this desire to create happiness and security for family and clan, is fuelled by the Ten of Cups imperative. What use is all of this if it doesn't make you and those you love happy? That imperative is what drives that fire, that Wands urge to create more, which in turn leads us to the creation of the new Ace that must inevitably follow if this legacy is to continue. That Wands desire to continue to create and build is managed and sustained through a healthy dose of mental acuity, intelligence and objectivity. The ability to face and overcome challenges and difficulty are vital ingredients if this experience is going to be maintained over time.

Chapter 25

A Personal Reading

I have been working on this book now for over a year and it's been a fascinating and challenging experience. As I am nearing the end of the writing process, I thought it would be interesting to see what the reading had to say about where 'we' are in things. My Question: 'What do I need to know about the next stage of finishing this book?' My 'You Are Here' card: the Three of Pentacles.

I'm still very much doing it 'like a job'; I'm in the process of implementing the plan but it isn't me doing this alone, there is a team involved. There are the kind folks who have been giving me feedback on text, proofreading, editing and creating artwork, but there is also the team of energetic guides who have been directing the content. We're all playing our part and doing our jobs. This is a very practical part, but still in the early stages of development as we can see from the fact it is a Three.

My Royal Significator Is the Page of Pentacles

Curious and future-orientated, this Page loves to learn about how to create the abundant life experience promised by the Ten of Pentacles. Learning, planning, studying process and 'how to do it' are this Page's interests. He loves the discovery for its own sake. Also, it's rather apt, as one of the themes of this book is that the Ten of Pentacles is actually the aspiration of the entire process; so my role as the exploratory Page, learning academically about how to reach the Ten of Pentacles, is perfect.

Guidance for My Area of Primary Focus? The Moon (Internal Process)

So I must focus on my own internal process as a way of moving to the next stage. The Moon is referring directly to an experience I'm having (the Moon being in the Experience Realm). The first thing that comes to mind is, I haven't been able to see the system or where the book is heading in its entirety next until the last minute. It's very much been a voyage of discovery that has revealed itself in the process of writing and experimentation. That's all been quite daunting to walk through. Being in the dark about the way forward is never easy, but when it describes an entire project it's even more challenging. Trusting the process and continuing to allow it to unfold has been all I have been able to do.

I must be able to play my part and uphold my end of the project to make things work. If I allow any fear to control the situation, I may end up not progressing the book project as I should.

The Page energy is encouraging me to be exploratory and curious. I must remember, there is joy and fascination in the process and all of this is learning and experience, on which I can continue to build beyond this project.

Also, perhaps I feel less than certain about some aspects of the book. How much to spend financially is uncertain, but also, how I'm going to explain the theories. Maybe I haven't adequately explained parts, or over-complicated others? I won't know until I've put words on paper and then committed to sending the book out into the world.

Extended Reading

I'll take a look at the cards along the Minor Arcana process. This tells me where I've been and where I'm going next. The card has placed me at the Three. I am to the left of the Six (the tipping point between stages). This tells me I am in the first stage of the Pentacles process. The Three of Pentacles acknowledges the fact that I am doing practical work right now also, as previously mentioned, that I'm not alone in the process. I have others around me who are adding their skills and experience. The Three looks right. Having established my idea for The Life Code deck and the book (the Ace), I have come out of the Two of Pentacles, plate-spinning and splitting my attention between those different projects and my private clients, teaching and readings. It places me right before the Four and Five of Pentacles in the process, so I need to stabilise further, bring everything to a point. The temptation of the Four of Pentacles is to be overly cautious I might play things too safe.

The number Four in Tarot refers to a stable base from which to build, bringing everything together to a point. Having done that, the temptation might be to avoid risking too much. The Five of Pentacles is scared, lacking in abundance or perhaps in confidence. There is much to risk, putting something new out into the world. This is where the fear may well come into effect. Also, how much do I want to invest financially? It also looks like resources are possibly something I need to consider next. How much will everything cost? I can see how the next stage carries its own problems and it tells me where I might hit road blocks in making it happen.

The Moon as my primary focus is supported by the other Majors in the Experience Realm.

Guidance to Staying on Track

The Star is very much the ground on which I am building — positivity, faith and hope. This project is one that is full of hope and is very much a star that I am following. The card tells me I am moving in the right direction, though, and to trust myself and the process. This is vital if I am to build from here. There are no guarantees and there will certainly be challenges ahead, but the signs are good. The book itself is about hope, the foundational ideal that we have power over ourselves and our life outcome. Trusting the process would be the ideal that I have been following out of necessity from the beginning.

The Sun, as a regulation, reminds me that I am supposed to be enjoying the project for itself. This is something I'm passionate about, after all. The enjoyment that the Page gets from learning is important but so is having fun around the situation. Lighten up, enjoy it. Stop taking things so seriously. Perhaps it's also a message from spirit to remember that things will become clear as the book progresses. The fact it has not been possible to see everything at once has been disconcerting and this has very much controlled the process of writing. I am being regulated by how much I can see at a time. I have had to trust that all will become clear as things progress.

Guidance for the Road Ahead

Wisdom as guidance around external factors — I guess it's telling me that the experience and judgements of others will be a factor in the next stage and that's something I can't control. I think this book presents some interesting ideas regarding some elements of the Tarot structure. How relevant these new ideas are deemed to be is yet to be known — that would definitely classify as 'external factors', relevant on the road ahead. From a personal perspective, I have travelled a very long road to get here and there have definitely been some tough lessons to learn along the way. I hope this card is telling me that I have gained enough experience to make this project all that I want it to be.

The World as a guiding principle is rather reassuring, but also reminds me that this phase (and all phases) must be successfully completed before I can progress to the next one. It's also important to know what 'successfully completed' means in this situation. What would 'success' look like? Completing the book is my main goal right now. I'm having some trouble looking beyond that so, right now, completion means success.

Finally, the Rod gives us the process by which the Moon card itself is constructed.

Death supports the process of moving through the dark environment that the Moon presents us with by assuring us that it's OK, change is good and in order for things to change we must also be prepared to change. Death tells us that what we think about change and endings will strongly influence our ability to adapt in the future. Relating to the reading, what about when the writing bit of the project ends and I must confront the next harder part, of getting this book out into the world? How I use my mind to navigate through the ending of the writing process into the next arguably harder part of the project will be pivotal.

Strength in the Energetic Realm supports the journey through the Moon by reminding us (me) to use my courage and determination to resolutely bring myself back to centre and find my way back to balance, when I notice that I am feeling uncomfortable.

Being uncomfortable is OK. Sometimes we must deal with our own fear or discomfort and not try to avoid it or react to it. We can view it with curiosity (Page energy) and learn from it. I am doing this because I want to build something; there is a point to it and it won't be forever. Being able to experience fear is important and how well I manage to deal with any feelings of insecurity on any level will show up in the results.

The Empress in the Emotional Realm is Ground Zero when it comes to dealing with fear of any kind. She represents our ability to know that we can take care of ourselves emotionally and physically through difficulty. As foundational advice on a creative project, she is of course, perfect. She reminds me that I (we all) are an endless well of creative energy and can always create again and again; it won't run out and there is always more to find.

These questions have encouraged me to step back and get some perspective on the process of writing. I loved the avatar of the Page of Pentacles: the picture of him sitting on his books, surrounded by knowledge and wisdom, researching, wondering and studying for the love of his subject. I found that comforting. It reminded me I have nothing to prove and that I would learn as much in the process as I would teach with the writing itself.

The gentle advice of the Major Arcana Experience Realm felt exactly right. The hope and optimism this book has engendered, the joy of discovery, the feeling that at times I was finding the way through, discovering more about the system and process incrementally along the way, only seeing the part that was important at the time and then the feeling of 'oh wow – I see something new', has been wonderful to experience. Knowing from past projects that the creative part is, in reality (however difficult it might seem at the time), actually the easy bit. Deciding how to move forward in the next stage will be a whole other decision making process, and deciding when it's done and that it is successful *because* it's done, is actually a big deal and something to be proud of.

Chapter 26

The Five Key Experiences – Going Deeper

The five key experiences refer to the five final cards of the Major Arcana, which fall into the Realm of Pentacles. These five cards give us the five key experiences that are the building blocks on which our life experience is created, which we now know are:

1. The Star = the experience of trust
2. The Moon = the experience of fear
3. The Sun = the experience of joy
4. Wisdom = the experience of action taken
5. The World = the experience of success

We must build a solid foundation on each of these experiences in turn, if we are to successfully create that rich abundant Ten of Pentacles destination.

Our exploration of the Tarot matrix so far has been along each of the horizontal axes, exploring the Realms of each suit individually. But, as we have seen from the readings in each Realm, we can also read the matrix vertically from top to bottom, through each Realm in turn to the Realm of Experience along the bottom line. As we have already established, the way we create our rich Pentacles abundance experience is the way we use and combine the other three suits. So, if we follow the five columns up from the final Realm through Swords and Wands back to Cups, we can unpack the components of those five key experiences. In this way, the matrix gives us not only the experiences themselves but also tells us how we can create them.

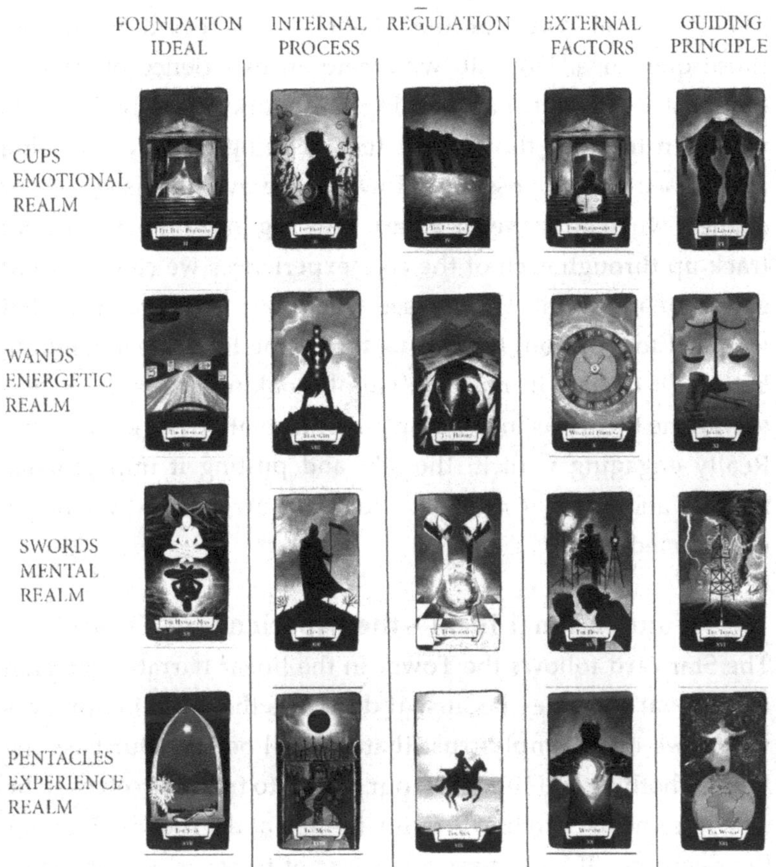

Why Is This Important?

In my readings with clients, some of the questions and statements that come up regularly are:

- How can I ever trust again?
- I lost my trust in myself, how can I know if anything will be OK ever again?
- I'm just too scared of the pain.
- How could I even risk going through that again?
- I don't know how to create a joyful life. I don't see how anything can change.

The five final cards of the Major Arcana begin to answer those questions. How do we create an experience of trust in ourselves? Without that, nothing will work properly. How do we begin to move though our fear of being hurt or not being able to see what's possible? How can we even envisage joy or change, when all we see is a dark grey fog in front of us? As we track up through each of the core experiences we can see what each is made up of. We can see where our gaps are and what we need to work on. It gives us the recipe to create something better. Of course, in real life, simply looking at the cards and seeing the theory as interesting and informative is a good thing. Really engaging with it, though, and putting it into practice is quite another. For now, let's look at how each experience is constructed.

Foundational Ideal – the Experience of Trust

The Star card follows the Tower in the linear narrative version of the Fool's Journey because it describes the point in our lives where we must simply trust that we will be OK. Our baseline faith in both us and life itself, our ability to trust ourselves to be able to come back to life, is quite literally at the root of all of our life decisions. If we experience a loss of trust, or perhaps have never really understood what it means, we can find ourselves having no faith at all that we will be OK, or that we will ever find a way through. Then we find ourselves stuck, unable or unwilling to create new, more positive experiences for fear of more pain. We simply cannot find our way through fear if we have no experience of trust that we can call on. The problem comes when we have placed all our trust in another person. When we do that, we are giving that other person responsibility for our lives and our ultimate happiness. This severely limits our own potential for creativity and stops us from being able to flow with life, and its ability to work with us energetically.

The Star is fuelled at its root by the High Priestess in that ever-foundational Emotional Realm, representing our connection to our own internal world, our knowledge of ourselves and who we really are. We are both light and shadow, but when we can bring both together into a powerful whole, not hiding bits of us away, we start to better understand our true nature.

We can embrace the Magician archetype, knowing that we can always create new experiences because we have faith in and trust our own core nature to do so. This engages the Chariot energy, which sets us free from the agendas of others, fuels our courage and our drive to take action in life. We are not pulled off course by fear or disillusionment.

This enables the Hanged Man energy. We are now able to sacrifice the old version of ourselves for a new version, one with a different perspective. The Hanged Man also advises patience, but this doesn't happen overnight; it takes time and investment.

The Star gives us respite from whatever it is we've gone through. It is a time to regroup, to start to feel better. It is within this process that we can start to see things differently. The Star asks us to trust the process, allowing life to do its work. To do that, though, we must trust the in-between stage. This is the quiet place where change happens, where we put some distance between us now and what's gone before; only then can we find our new beginning. This is the foundational ideal on which all experiences are built on.

Internal Process — the Experience of Fear

The Moon is the internal process we must go through in order to create new and better experiences for ourselves. To be able to experience our fear and deal with our trauma we must first build on the Star foundation of trust. The Moon represents our experience of not being able to see clearly. It also refers to our shadow side, the darkness we fear inside ourselves. Being able to move through and not be afraid of the dark, whether it be internal or external, is vital if we want to be able to recreate ourselves and our lives effectively. If we explore the three cards in column two, we will see how powerfully they each help us do exactly that, and how a strong foundational internal support system enables that process.

Our relationship with the Empress card, with its message of us being fertile ground and our ability to love and nurture ourselves through hard times, gives us the starting point for our ability to withstand the discomfort of fear. Fear causes an energetic disturbance within us, but if we can focus our courage and creative energy within, we can bring ourselves back into balance. To be able to move beyond endings and to deal with grief and heartache is a strength that is hard won; we fear loss most powerfully, but if we can accept that endings are a part of life and necessary for new birth, then we can trust ourselves to find our way back to the light.

Death, as an archetype, represents that loss which we fear most but, having made peace with the idea of allowing all change, we can confront it and any other fear from a different perspective. Our instinct is often to try and avoid our greatest fears, but if we can meet them head on, we find we are liberated from their limitations and are free to recreate whenever we need to, living life at its fullest expression.

If we can see ourselves as someone for whom this is possible, we will have a powerful, internal process at our disposal that will mean we can trust ourselves to be able to deal with almost anything. Then we can approach life with more confidence and certainty and fear will not be running the show or driving the metaphorical bus.

The Experience of Joy — Regulation

The Sun, with its message of joy, is built on grittier foundations than perhaps we would first imagine. This joy is not a fluffy bunny, floaty vision of happiness that comes from nowhere or just 'happens' to us if we're lucky. It's the result of some serious decision making. Deciding what your parameters are and what is OK and not OK for you is not always an easy task. We can only do this effectively if we have first laid the groundwork of the first two experiences (the Star and the Moon). The trust we have in ourselves and our ability to deal with our fear of loss are what makes it possible to draw our lines in the sand. If we're afraid that saying no will mean we lose love, then we must go back to Moon, track back to the Empress and redo the work there.

Having effective boundaries means not giving other people 'the wheel' in your life. The ability to say, 'that's enough', and mean it, can be life-changing. Having some self-discipline and some structure brings self-respect. This then gives you a sense that you can support yourself without the need for others to prop you up. You are self-reliant, confident and independent.

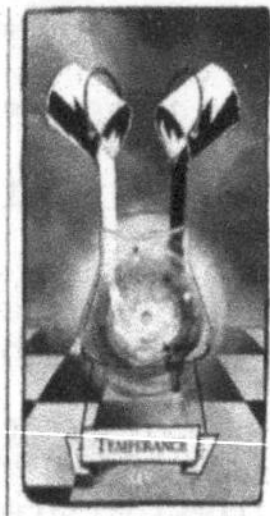

This gives you the ability to create the right balance for you. It puts you squarely at the centre of your own experience.

You are the magician in your life, and you must take responsibility for the mixture of ingredients you have allowed in and your use of them. It's not an exact science, but when we get it right, the life experience we can create is limitless. Of course, it's an ongoing process; we must constantly re-balance and re-position. The mix is constantly changing, and we must decide how much and in what way we change with it. Once we are free from the fear of abandonment, failure and not being good enough, we can see ourselves in the light of our true potential. We are free to create a rich and confident life experience that doesn't just 'happen' and doesn't crumble in the face of disappointment. The Sun experience is where we see life and ourselves clearly; this fills us full of energy and enthusiasm – full of love, delighted with ourselves and life itself.

External Factors – Experience of Experiences

Wisdom, with its message of 'good judgement', is built on our experience of life so far. Every time we take an action and have a subsequent experience we grow and learn, amassing those experiences into a rulebook for life. Wisdom, though, is the ability to reassess those experiences and judge them in hindsight with insight and compassion, enabling us to make better, more informed decisions moving forward.

We begin building our initial knowledge from the foundational ground of the culture in which we were raised. This often is first evident when we are confronted with the contrast between family and school. What our early experiences of acceptance were and whether we fitted in or not, The rules of the society in which we first live form the bedrock of who we think we are, in relation to the world in which we live. As we try out aspects of ourselves in response to these rules, what comes back from those experiments starts to form our first belief systems about who we are in the hierarchy of life, and gives us the sense of self and the face with which we approach the world.

Then we are again tested at the next level by the more unpredictable forces of life itself and its often seemingly capricious tendency to knock us off our perches. We then take our initial decisions about our position in the hierarchy and our identity and, as life spins around us, we respond as we instinctively see fit. These further experiments give us yet more evidence as to the nature of life and how we can best navigate through.

Navigating life is a very tough learning curve though, and we learn pretty quickly that pain and disappointment is a part of life that is quite simply unavoidable, even given our absolute best try. It is in our attempts to avoid pain and discomfort that we are tempted by quick fix solutions to solve difficult problems. We often get hypnotised by solutions that seem like a really good idea at the time.

These solutions feel good in the moment, but just don't lead anywhere useful, ultimately sometimes causing more pain than we originally tried to avoid. The Devil card describes a limited vision of what is possible in life. It is 'Fake Love'! The desire here is to make ourselves feel better, and we disappear out of the light and into the shadows to do it — this is very much a solo show and takes care of no one but ourselves in the process.

Still, we learn though (hopefully), and the information that we get from encountering ourselves in these situations tells us who we think we are in life. This last bit of experience is almost the most important. The Devil card shines a light on what we believe to be true about life and ourselves, and that information will go a long way to deciding our 'fate'. Mistakes are really not terminal though, especially when we view them from the position of being made from the lack of a better experience. In that light, they can actually become vital components in the story. They are experiential gifts for us; they will, if we allow them to, add to our wealth of experience, ultimately making us richer as a result. Wisdom is gained as a result of us living a life rich in experience, both of the light and the dark of life and ourselves, which means we can apply that 'good judgement' to whatever we decide to create, moving forward.

Guiding Principle — the Experience of Success

As a guiding principle, the World card asks us to be guided by what we consider 'success' to be. The World represents the culmination of everything coming together: our emotional, energetic and mental skills creating experiences that add richness and success to our lives.

It is where our mastery of life's creative skills is as good as it gets from the perspective of our current standpoint. In this model, the World is not a destination of spiritual mastery, it is advice about your Ten of Pentacles aspiration. It tells you must own your experience of your world as it is, because this is what you have created.

As the final card of the five key Pentacles experiences we must have in our quest of the Ten of Pentacles, it asks us what our experience of 'success' now is, and what we want it to be in the future. Success is an important experience. If we don't know what success feels like, how will we even know what our version might look like? How will we know what choices to make for future success?

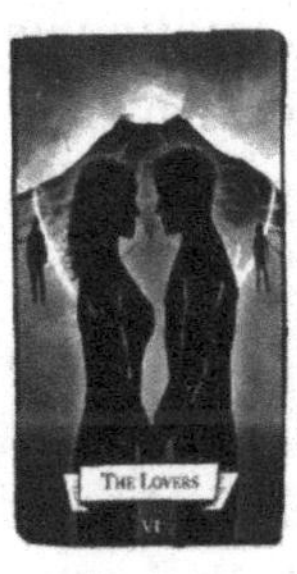

We have free will, which hands us the power to make choices for ourselves. That choice normally sits between Love, and its arch nemesis, Fear. This really is fundamental if we look at what true success is really built on. To choose love is not a matter of romance, it's a matter of courage. The Lovers card asks us: what do you love? If we see the Ten of Cups (happiness, connectedness and fulfilment) as the fuel that is driving almost all of our decision making, the choices we make in the Lovers card will be at the very heart of our 'World' vision. Every choice we make has consequences, and what we base our choices on, what we decide we love more, will show up as evidence in the results of what we have created. On examining the evidence, we must make a judgement. Perhaps the consequences of our choices have not led to the successful outcome first envisaged? Perhaps things didn't work out as we thought they would do. Now we are faced with the realisation that what we built with the choices we made just didn't stand up. Then we must choose again; the Tower card in Tarot forces us to re-evaluate everything in our life.

Our original choices in the Lovers were made because of things we probably believed to be true but, in the light of the evidence, perhaps we are being invited to reconsider: who are we? What do we believe in now? What do we actually want? What is fair, what isn't and what do we do about it? How much power do we actually have?

The Tower levels the ground on which we stand, inviting us to rebuild a new, more successful world for ourselves, which in itself again brings us full circle – refining those core experiences offered by the Star, the Moon and then the Sun.

The Magician's pursuit of mastery refers to us as we learn about the true nature of what we are capable of, all of it – all of us. Only by really knowing ourselves can we know what power we really have at our disposal to create and shape that Ten of Pentacles life experience. A life that is ultimately rich and fulfilling, not just for us but also for those we care about.

Chapter 27

In Conclusion: A Map of How to Do Life

About halfway through the process of creating The Life Code deck and the Tarot course for Gayle's client, I became aware that I was seeing Tarot in a very different way. It was emerging for me as a complete philosophy, and one with a very distinct character. The overall system and the matrix within it had emerged as a set of parameters by which we can measure ourselves and see where we are in all things. The guidance was laser-focussed towards a very clear goal. However, unlike other spiritual disciplines which are perhaps more angled towards specifically spiritual aspirations, this was focussed very much on making our human life better, in the here and now, fully conversant with the entire spectrum of human nature; our light and our dark, our turbulent emotions, our frailties and our capacity for creativity and incredible courage.

The purpose was not to become less human – spiritual for its own sake – but to use love, our desire for happiness and our human desire to build our own design. To create an improved environment for everyone. In many other spiritual practices, we are often encouraged to detach from the here and now, to see this life as merely temporary, something to be endured, seeing ourselves as flawed and perhaps even beyond help. This philosophy has a different take on all of this.

This life may well be temporary, but it's important. What we do here changes things; what we are learning and experiencing changes things. We are here to live and experience life to the fullest. The suit of Pentacles has the aspiration of a rich abundant life, but one built on the foundation of love, stability and security. In order to make things better for us all, we must start with ourselves; the better we build, the bigger the ripples are through time and space. The Tarot philosophy of life is incredibly proactive, and the Magician (AKA us) is the conduit through which spirit works.

But we also have spirit within us; it is the divine part of us which connects to the energetic world and by which we can create our life experience. The more effectively and confidently we take control of our life experience, the better and more joyful life gets.

This is not about trying to avoid pain, or difficulty or temptation, it's about learning what we and life have to offer; dancing and flowing with it.

Also, it's not just us that is doing the creating here, we are co-creating with the power of our connection to the energetic world, constantly attracting elements and shaping our external life experience, whether we know it or not. What is possible depends on the limitations we ourselves put on it.

Ultimately, the goal is to regulate our lives through the lens of joy so we can see life clearly, without fear. Becoming enlightened by default, by doing and experiencing, not by abstinence, design or desire. Enlightenment is simply being able to see the truth; to see through the veil of the illusions of fear as spirit does. It's not easy, it takes 10,000 hours to be a master at anything after all, but it's worth it.

Life is an amazing gift right here, right now and the real sin is not to live it to our fullest potential.

Sitting in the car all those years ago, I had no idea how to 'do life'. It seemed like a cruel impenetrable mystery. I asked for a map, and this is it. I hope you have found it as fascinating as I have; I hope it sparks something in you that makes a real difference to your life.

Epilogue

Who Is Obin?

Obin is the name of the team of guides that started working with me just before the idea for The Life Code deck surfaced. The subsequent work we started to do together stood out as markedly different from the way I had been working before. Readings became more like channelled deliveries. Clients started to appear who all had very similar issues and I realised that some of the ideas that were emerging through the process of creating the deck and the course, were absolutely in tune with the help that those clients needed. In all that time though, I never thought to question or investigate the name Obin itself.

About ten days ago I decided to ask during a meditation why they had given me that name to identify them with.

'Because that's who we are', came the reply from a distinctly female voice.

I was intrigued though, so I decided to investigate further and with the help of my friend and numerological specialist Kay Kraty, this is what I discovered.

Numerology breaks a name down into different parts.

Vowel Sounds create the soul urge in a name — O (h) and I (sound non-capital I) — 'Soul Urge' refers to your true motivation, the bigger picture behind what is driving your choices.

Consonants create the personality. B and N — Personality refers to the enduring characteristics and behaviour, including major traits, values, self-concept, abilities, and emotional patterns.

Vowel *O* Resonates at 15/6

The O is the voice of creation, and it is linked to God energy, Source Energy, solar energy. It also refines and clarifies information, frequencies and vibration so that is acceptable to receive for those who need it. Because the O is an open sound, it can carry on forever, it is a limitless energy. Because we (physical) are not functioning on that God vibration, we can only take tiny little bits of that, and it has to be sort of filtered down so that we can actually comprehend it.

It's very much an energy for service and doing something for the whole, for humanity rather than for the individual. However, in numerology everything has two sides, and it has within it the potential for both positive and negative, for light and for dark. Creation Source Energy is everything. It's not just everything that's perfect.

The number 15 in Tarot refers to the Devil card and the 6 in Tarot refers to a tipping point, the balance between stages of ways of being. Creative energy is all things, so has the potential for very high energy, which you could call angelic, and the opposite, much lower vibration which might be referred to as the devil energy. But you could argue, both are necessary, because we cannot uplift what we don't understand in terms of our shadow cells. So you would need something that would be able to delve deep into the darkness in order to bring light into it.

It is the number of choice – you choose either one or the other. That doesn't mean that you have to stay in that choice though; it's a presentation of all possibilities which are then expressed into our life as experiences.

If we understand 15/6 as the voice of creation, it tells us that the way we express ourselves is what is being called into being. And it very much chimes in with that old biblical premise, in the beginning was the word. It is what we bring into being by what we communicate into the space.

The number 6 reminds us that it's all about balance, learning how to deal with extremes but also learning how to balance all the elements of ourselves in order to ultimately get to a point of perfection. The suggestion is, that in order to do that, we need to stay in the energy of love because that is the only actual place we have where we can observe everything with equanimity, with compassion, and see it for what it is.

Vowel *I* Resonates at 18/9

So the next open sound is the I (i) of Obin. And that resonates to an 18/9.

Number 18, as one of the sacred numbers in Hebrew, represents life itself and in Pythagoras numerology, 9 speaks of transformation and transition. It carries at its core the energy of regeneration. There is a powerful teaching element within this number, The intention here is to guide and transform, without expecting anything in return. It is teaching from the perspective of learning to take responsibility. The words sainthood, sacrifice and martyr are also heavily significant in this energy implying that there is suffering involved within the process of regeneration. The suffering occurs because of attachment to the illusions of physical life. The teaching is to enable a breakdown of falsehood and limitation which are at the root of the suffering, a process which can be in and of itself, challenging. The regeneration aspect is to enable the creation of a more spiritualised self. This can be a process that will bring about some painful realisations which then lead to a transition. The guidance is not about avoiding suffering but learning from it. For the pupil to sacrifice themselves as they once were. The word sacrifice means to make something sacred. In service of that goal, that teaching is given freely and with a love of humanity. For the highest good of all, to raise up the whole to a higher level of understanding. A very high frequency energy that is about compassion and selfless service.

Combining the *O* and the *I* together

The O and the I are both open vowel sounds; they're both soul energies which, when combined, give the total soul urge of the name Obin. This total is associated with the Christ vibration, the Christ flame. It refers to a very high frequency that is about compassion and selfless service.

And so it has within its name, the energy of the Saviour. That particular number, 33, is called the Saviour because it has the urge and the ability to save people. It's a reformer by nature. In other words, it will take something and change it; you could say transmute it or transform it.

It's an energy that very much champions the underdog. People who are bereft, the 'have nots' of the world, people who are poor in all manner of ways. In love, in confidence, in knowledge and understanding, in financial abundance in whatever ways they are lacking, this is the energy that is there for them.

The whole of this soul urge number is also about discerning right from wrong, keeping on track, doing it for others, service to the community, creating and choosing. It facilitates an awareness of the choices that are available, so that you learn the choices that will benefit you instead of the choices you made previously that are not in your interest, if you want things to change.

Consonants *B* and *N* – Personality of Obin

Consonants are closed sounds; energetically separate, you can't string them out forever. They have cut off because they're separate; they resonate with the idea of personality not soul. This is the description of how the energy thinks of itself.

The B is just a straightforward 2. And the 2 resonates quite straightforwardly with 'ray of love and wisdom'. It also resonates with water. It's very receptive. It's the mother, the nurturer, it has that feminine energy. It's also the measurer. If you measure something, you have one end and you have the other end. So again, it demonstrates polarity — it has extremes — one or the other, both possibilities. But its instinct is unification. While a very similar energy to the vowel sounds, it very much has its feet on the ground. It's a very much more earthy energy because it is a consonant and also because it's a much lower number.

The number 2 is on the first spiral of numbers — the first spiral being 1 to 9. So as the ray of love and wisdom, it is defined as pure love energy. Because it is the measurer and because it is receptive, it nurtures its whole space. It holds the space for stuff to unfold. And so it's the energy that holds everything together. It's also about protection and self-protection. But then on the other side (because it is everything and all encompassing) it could be overprotective, potentially strangling the thing it loves. So, if this is an overriding consciousness, it must be able to allow humanity to be fallible.

The number 2 is about self-mastery on the emotional plane. And that may well be what it is trying to help create for humanity, because humans find emotional self-mastery very challenging.

Okay, so we go now to the N, which is the final letter of this word and the last letter that relates to the personality.

The N is a 5, but that is generated from the number 23. So it's a 23/5 which is a double digit, which is then brought together into a single digit. The 5 is a master communicator, expressing and communicating ideas in ways that are easy to understand. Spiritually, the 5 is an alchemist who can connect the 5 worlds: the physical, etheric, astral, mental, and causal planes. Its name is Peter Pan. Now, Peter Pan, as you might recall, never wanted to grow old, he just wanted to keep playing in the sun. At its highest level, this is a very uplifting number. It is a key to the sun, how to dance with the sun, how to always be in that light. The sun is symbolic of the higher light, the light with the capital L.

At a lower level, this is a risk-taking energy. Peter Pan energy doesn't like to have any limitations; again, at this lower frequency, it could even be seen as reckless. Why? It's an energy that wants to be in motion, not bound by limitations. But also free from self-will and to come from a place where, quoting the Bible, it's not my will, but thy will be done. In other words, everything I do, I do with a consciousness that I'm a vehicle for something. That doesn't mean choices aren't made. They very much are, but they are made with a responsibility with the best of intentions, and with an understanding of the impact of those beyond itself.

The combined number of the personality is 25/7. Its name is the birth of consciousness.

The birth of consciousness has a huge spectrum in terms of frequency and uplift. The 2 and the 7 of 25/7 both resonate with emotion. It is the need for the consciousness to birth at the emotional level. For one to become emotionally conscious and again, finding the rudder that we all have for our emotions and then steering and choosing those emotions. It's a great manifesto of feelings – from feeling down and disengaged to the heights of the archetypal drama queen and fusing the use of breadth of knowledge of that to help others. The 25 /7 birth of consciousness is at the bottom line; the bringer in of the light of truth and it is the number of the mind going into emotion.

OBIN – Overall Self-Expression 22/4 (soul urge + personality)

The 22 is known as a Master Builder. This energy refers to the energy that feeds in between the 22, expanding it out. It is an energy of mastery. There is no middle ground. If the previous level was the CEO, this is like chairman of the board level. This is much further up. It is creating something in your mind or your consciousness or your awareness and then making it happen. The Master Builder is building on the spiritual plane; it's about spiritualising matter and everyday life. So ideally, it's about turning dreams into reality. It is creating something in your mind or your consciousness or your awareness and then making it happen.

4 is the number that grounds and stabilises the 22 energies. So, at its highest level, it's about creation. It's about creating something real, from just something floating. Bringing it into being, from an idea into form. Enabling the structure, giving it edges and corners, making it into matter, giving it endurance, it is very practical in nature. It makes things viable; it is, in effect, the blueprint of the divine.

That stabilisation the 4 brings also invites the polarity of attachment and detachment. The ability to go into the dark to release fear. The square shape allows you the security to sink; to go further down into the darkness and to do the work needed to transmute, to release and let go, learning to be flexible, but keeping your feet on the ground. And you do all this at the highest point, from a point of unconditional love, which is giving without expectation of return. Manifesting from the dark to the light.

Viewing all this through the lens of Tarot, I found it all absolutely fascinating. We already understand the number 4 represents a firm foundation from which to build; it is the place from which to work out our patterns from the obstacles of poverty, heartache and failure (which we encounter in the Minor Arcana number 5). 4 is the place where energy becomes grounded; it is 'down to earth' in essence and is therefore associated with home, stability, security, and contentment. This is a perfect description of the system as a whole, which is focussed on how to create the Ten of Pentacles as the primary goal, creating a rich, sustainable, secure happy life.

But what about 22, what is the relevance of that?

There are 22 cards in the Major Arcana but no card number 22. We get to number 22 because the Fool card begins the cycle at 0; the World card is number 21.

The first number of the Major Arcana is 1, represented by the Magician; this is the point at which the energy becomes manifested. The Fools Journey takes him through all 21 Major Arcana cards, returning once more to number 1, the Magician. The energy that powers the Magician is infinite, it is a cycle that never ends. The Fool in his positions at both the beginning and the end of the Major Arcana, are in effect both 0 and 22.

This cyclic pattern runs through all of Tarot – through the Minor Arcana as well as the Majors.

The Minor Arcana starts its journey at 23 with the Ace of Cups, (if we use The Life Code system) and continues on to card 78, thus ending with the Ten of Pentacles as the final card, which is the culmination of the Tarot Journey.

The Fool as 0 represents the energy of all potential (all the Tarot Aces).

The cycle is infinite – there is no ending, no limit to the creative potential of the Fool or source energy within it. The number 22 is also the ancient numerical symbol for a circle, representing both the Alpha and Omega, described in the Christian Bible as God himself.

I also loved the number 2 in the personality section. This resonates beautifully in Tarot energy with the Empress card (no. 2). She, as the archetypal mother, is very much the crucible of unconditional love. When we look at her role in the Emotional Realm, as the very earth from which all love and creativity comes, the personality of Obin makes perfect sense.

On the few occasions when I have had direct contact with Obin outside of the Tarot, it has been a specifically female energy that has been communicating. I think I first encountered her when I was studying channelling (trance mediumship) at The Arthur Findlay college. To be honest I wasn't finding much success in allowing spirit to use me to speak through. I just felt dizzy and felt like I was in a fog of some kind.

The Tutor made a direct request to Spirit to show me, and what happened next was a massive physical sensation that a huge energy of unconditional love had joined with me. It was like being one with it. It's a difficult thing to describe, so all-encompassing was it. It was disorientating for a few seconds then of course, I wanted to stay with it permanently. Reading the description above of who Obin is, I am not at all surprised that the energy felt so unutterably beautiful.

As I have been working on this project, my friend Ray has been asking me periodically, 'Yes all the theory works, but what is it for?' I haven't, in all truth, been able to answer that. I think the description of Obin is the answer to that question. It seems fitting it has come right at the end of the book. She (they) want to help, and have given us this system as a way of understanding Tarot slightly differently. As a way of helping us move through the blocks that are stopping us from being happy. I think it is a beautiful system, mathematical in its structure, as I guess exactly how it would be delivered by a Master Builder.

O-BOOKS

SPIRITUALITY

O is a symbol of the world, of oneness and unity; this eye represents knowledge and insight. We publish titles on general spirituality and living a spiritual life. We aim to inform and help you on your own journey in this life.
If you have enjoyed this book, why not tell other readers by posting a review on your preferred book site?

Recent bestsellers from O-Books are:

Heart of Tantric Sex
Diana Richardson
Revealing Eastern secrets of deep love and intimacy to Western couples.
Paperback: 978-1-90381-637-0 ebook: 978-1-84694-637-0

Crystal Prescriptions
The A-Z guide to over 1,200 symptoms and their healing crystals
Judy Hall
The first in the popular series of eight books, this handy little guide is packed as tight as a pill bottle with crystal remedies for ailments.
Paperback: 978-1-90504-740-6 ebook: 978-1-84694-629-5

Shine On

David Ditchfield and J S Jones

What if the after effects of a near-death experience were undeniable? What if a person could suddenly produce high-quality paintings of the afterlife, or if they acquired the ability to compose classical symphonies? Meet: David Ditchfield.

Paperback: 978-1-78904-365-5 ebook: 978-1-78904-366-2

The Way of Reiki

The Inner Teachings of Mikao Usui

Frans Stiene

The roadmap for deepening your understanding of the system of Reiki and rediscovering your True Self.

Paperback: 978-1-78535-665-0 ebook: 978-1-78535-744-2

You Are Not Your Thoughts

Frances Trussell

The journey to a mindful way of being, for those who want to truly know the power of mindfulness.

Paperback: 978-1-78535-816-6 ebook: 978-1-78535-817-3

The Mysteries of the Twelfth Astrological House

Fallen Angels

Carmen Turner-Schott, MSW, LISW

Everyone wants to know more about the most misunderstood house in astrology — the twelfth astrological house.

Paperback: 978-1-78099-343-0 ebook: 978-1-78099-344-7

Feng Shui Your Way to Abundance
Janine Lowe
Feng Shui Your Way to Abundance shows how to use Feng Shui to attract positive energy and change into your life.
Paperback: 978-1-80341-674-8 ebook: 978-1-80341-683-0

Naked in the Now
Marijke McCandless
What if getting present was less like work and more like being seduced by a lover?
Paperback: 978-1-80341-567-3 ebook: 978-1-80341-574-1

Crystal Creed
Jamie Inglett
A beginner's guide to learning the sacred healing powers of crystals
Paperback: 978-1-80341-438-6 ebook: 978-1-80341-439-3

Revealing Light
Maryann Weston
YouTube psychic-astrologer Maryann Weston, from Revealing Light, shares her spiritual evolution after cancer had activated dormant psychic gifts, revealing a new purpose...
Paperback: 978-1-80341-730-1 ebook: 978-1-80341-738-7

Temple of Love
Natalie Glebova
The secret to true love is closer than you think.
Paperback: 978-1-80341-784-4 ebook: 978-1-80341-810-0

Readers of ebooks can buy or view any of these bestsellers by clicking on the live link in the title. Most titles are published in paperback and as an ebook. Paperbacks are available in traditional bookshops. Both print and ebook formats are available online.

Find more titles and sign up to our readers' newsletter at **www.o-books.com**

Follow O-Books on Facebook at **O-Books**